Understanding God

UNDERSTANDING GOD

ᴄ The Key Issue in Present-Day Protestant Thought

FREDERICK HERZOG

CHARLES SCRIBNER'S SONS ᴄ New York

Copyright Notices and Acknowledgments

The author thanks the following publishers and copyright owners for per-
mission to reprint from the works indicated below:

FORTRESS PRESS and SCM PRESS Ltd—From *Word and Faith* by Gerhard
Ebeling.

HARCOURT, BRACE & WORLD, INC. and the ANN ELMO AGENCY—From *Selected Poems of Bertolt Brecht* translated by H. R. Hays. Copyright 1947 by
Bertolt Brecht and H. R. Hays.

HARPER & ROW, PUBLISHERS, INCORPORATED—From *The New Hermeneutic* edited by James M. Robinson and John B. Cobb, Jr. Copyright © 1964
by James M. Robinson.

JOHN KNOX PRESS and the CHRISTIAN CENTURY FOUNDATION—From "Creative Negation in Theology" by Thomas J. J. Altizer, *The Christian Century*
(July 7, 1965), included in a series, "How I Am Making Up My Mind," to
be printed in book form, 1967.

THE MACMILLAN COMPANY—From *The Secular City* by Harvey Cox. Copyright © 1965 by Harvey Cox.

THE WESTMINSTER PRESS and SCM PRESS LTD—From *The Honest to God
Debate* edited by David L. Edwards. Copyright © 1963 by SCM Press.

PREFACE

The book attempts to give an overview of the present debate in Protestant theology, focusing on the new quest of God. Theological issues of the new quest of the historical Jesus and the new hermeneutic, and ethical queries of the new morality and the secular city are viewed as integrally related to the new focus.

I see the limitations of understanding God. In an ultimate sense, his ways are past tracing out. Even so, in his unconcealment God invites us to rethink his ways within the limits of our understanding.

I wish to pay tribute to two men whose names will not appear on these pages otherwise, but who significantly contributed to the making of the book. During the writing Jean-Frédéric Oberlin was often "looking over my shoulder." More than anyone else in our so-called modern age, it was this patient deacon of Christ who taught me that theology today can hardly make sense except as diakonic theology. There was also the abiding influence of Abraham Lincoln, articulating for me the specifically political agony of modern life, so that the *diakonia* I now see emerging as crucible of theological thought is distinctly a *diakonia* in politics.

Facing God's *diakonia* in his Word compels us to face him in our slums and—in Vietnam. Facing God we realize we are responsible for both.

I am grateful to the publishers for their interest during the various stages of the book and keen reader critique. I owe a special word of thanks to my typist, Miss Bessie Chronaki, for meticulous work on the manuscript, and to my wife, Kristin, for continuing teamwork in the theological workshop without which this book would not be what it is. I am also indebted to my students who always keep me on my toes.

F. H.

January 1966

CONTENTS

-ᙅ VI ᙆ-
THE PRESENT-DAY TASK
OF SYSTEMATIC THEOLOGY

THE NEW QUEST OF GOD

> *I look at myself and see chest, thighs, feet—a head.*
> *This strange organization, I know it will die. And inside—*
> *something, something, happiness . . . "Thou movest me."*
> *. . . Is it an idiot joy that makes this animal, the most pe-*
> *culiar animal of all, exclaim something? And he thinks this*
> *reaction a sign, a proof, of eternity? And he has it in his*
> *breast? But I have no arguments to make about it. "Thou*
> *movest me."* [1]
>
> SAUL BELLOW

IN the first half of the sixties a number of books have appeared
in Protestant theology that have reoriented the theological debate.[2] After World War II the problem of demythologizing
caught the imagination of a large segment of Protestant theology.
In the early fifties this particular concern led to a new quest of
the historical Jesus.[3] From an examination of the Christian message the debate moved on to a new interest in the person to whom
the message refers. Recently Protestant theology has taken a
further step. It is now "rediscovering" the reality to which both
the Christian message and the historical Jesus point: the being
of God. The impact of John A. T. Robinson's *Honest to God*,
published in March 1963, can hardly be appreciated without
considering this development.

The new quest of God does not rule out continuing interest
in the other two concerns. But it makes them appear in a new
light. As early as 1941, Rudolf Bultmann concluded his essay on
demythologizing by suggesting that after the demythologization
of the mythological image of Jesus Christ some might still regard

an action of God as myth.[4] Perhaps all along this was the more fundamental issue. But now it had been articulated in an unmistakable way. Protestant theology would again know who God is, if he is at all.

Occasionally the situation in which we find ourselves is referred to as a "theological revolution." [5] For the purposes of our discussion it will suffice to say that the theological debate, at least in the United States, has found a new focus. Martin E. Marty and Dean G. Peerman, in their introduction to New Theology No. 2, have also sized up the focus in terms of a new concern for the problem of God: "Today more and more theologians are returning to the problem of God or, to be more precise, to the problem of the godless man. Anyone indexing recent theological literature is sure to be impressed by the sudden and dramatic return of this question to the tables of contents of the more influential journals." [6]

The comment of Marty and Peerman reflects some ambiguity in the new quest of God. The quest might even be understood as a concern for the problem of godless man if viewed from the perspective of some of the participants. A "death of God theology" has emerged that seems to surrender all interest in the being of God. In this respect there might be little sense in speaking of a new quest of God. But the "death of God" is understood in different ways. For some the acceptance of the "death of God" is merely a way of expressing the waiting for a new revelation of God. For others it is, as it were, the "thorn in the flesh" that presses them on to a new quest of God. The most moving voice in this respect is that of Langdon Gilkey. Writing in The Christian Century, February 3, 1965, on "Dissolution and Reconstruction in Theology," he asks: "Is the first commandment . . . a relic of another age, and is only the second left for us to ponder and follow?" Answering his own question, he claims: "Our primary problem is . . . to discover how the God who has almost disappeared may appear to us again in power and in truth. . . . We must have some certainty that there is a referent to our word 'God'. . . . no revelation, no Christ of faith, no ecclesiology is ultimately possible or intelligible if the category of deity remains totally empty." [7]

Apart from the common search for a referent [8] to the word "God," the present situation in Protestant systematic theology gives the impression of dissolution. Reflecting on the Second Consultation on Hermeneutics held at Drew University, April 9–11, 1964, Robert W. Funk writes: "It is as if, all of a sudden, the things our theological tradition took for granted can no longer be taken for granted. Reality as the post-war generation experiences it does not permit the easy affirmation of some traditional starting point, in relation to which the theological enterprise can be newly ordered; rather, it senses the necessity to take nothing as the presupposition (least of all God or faith) of its theological endeavor." [9] Funk makes it abundantly clear that in his view as well God has lost his fixed place: "It is not simply a matter of not assuming the Christian tradition, but of not assuming the God-hypothesis either." It is, however, precisely the "general disinclination to regard conventional God-language as meaningful" described by Funk, which confronts us with the problem articulated by Gilkey: What sense is there to speak of Christ or the church without admitting that Christ and the church want to point beyond themselves to God?

A search for God involves a hermeneutical query, man's quest as an understanding being. In particular, man wants to understand how he understands. Ernst Fuchs has said: "There is a hermeneutical principle for the utterance 'God,' so that one has to consider what is happening when a man uses this word." [10] *Understanding God* is a phrase that seeks to characterize the recent efforts of interpreting the word "God" together with the attempt to state our own position.

Understanding God implies a definite hermeneutic, a method of understanding. Langdon Gilkey believes that the "theological question about God precedes the hermeneutical [question]." [11] Actually the theological question about God *is* a hermeneutical question: How can we understand God as the referent of language about God? The stress on *hermeneutic* in this context suggests that God is not a scientific problem in terms of the objectifying thought still widely prevalent in natural science. H. P. Rickman, in his introduction to Wilhelm Dilthey, *Pattern and Meaning in History*, makes the point that hermeneutic presupposes a "decisive difference between the natural sciences and the human studies." Understanding relates to "something much more simple and fundamental" than objectifying knowledge.[12] Wilhelm Dilthey defined hermeneutic as interpretation: "Interpretation would be impossible if expressions of life were completely strange. It would be unnecessary if nothing strange were in them. It lies, therefore, between these two extremes. It is always required where something strange is to be grasped through the art of understanding."[13] In this vein the theological question about God as a hermeneutical question asks whether the word "God" relates to some aspect of human experience: Is language about God completely strange to man? The hermeneutical question relative to God wants to understand in what sense it is true that God is, as theology claims. It wants to understand this primarily on the level of non-objectifying thought.

Gerhard Ebeling has asserted that understanding comes *through* language. *"The primary phenomenon in the realm of understanding is not understanding OF language, but understanding THROUGH language."*[14] But even if language could create understanding, it always addresses itself to man's experience. The question is whether God is completely strange to man's experience. Is there any awareness in man's experience of the reality to which the word "God" refers? In this respect the emphasis on hermeneutic tries to establish that Christianity is a truth claim and not merely a language game. Theological hermeneutic seeks to check the reality claims of the Christian faith.

The new quest of God is evolving at a time when the hermeneutical concern has received a new emphasis, summed up in the phrase "the new hermeneutic."[15] Thus far both concerns have not been coordinated to any appreciable extent. If the new hermeneutic would center in on the understanding of God, its reflections would be more clearly focused. If the new quest of God would relate itself to the new hermeneutic, it could interpret its search more intelligibly in the context of the Christian memory.

We are not assuming that we will perfect a union of the new quest of God and the new hermeneutic. But we can at least try to point out the direction in which further work in systematic theology might be pursued. Our concern for the new quest of

God in terms of hermeneutic means that we are trying to focus on the *method* of various forms of understanding God in present-day Protestantism while at the same time articulating our own method. We use the word "hermeneutic" to characterize the method of *understanding* over against an epistemology, a theory of knowledge. Our book does not intend to develop a comprehensive theological hermeneutic. It will deal chiefly with the primal components of theological understanding as they function methodologically. In view of the methodological concern we will occasionally speak of our own effort and its New Testament model as a *hermeneutic of God*, especially in order to distinguish it from a hermeneutic of faith.[16]

When we call attention to a new quest of God, we see its predecessor in the development culminated by Rudolf Otto's *The Idea of the Holy* (1917). The starting point of the old quest of God was Schleiermacher's treatise *On Religion: Speeches to Its Cultured Despisers* (1799). Although there have been numerous doctrines of God since Rudolf Otto's day, the examination of the concept of God was not central. In the early twenties, dialectical theology discussed the question of God vigorously. But God did not become the central theme in terms of a quest.

The *New Essays in Philosophical Theology*, published by Antony Flew and Alasdair MacIntyre in 1955, might prove to have been the forerunner of the new quest of God.[17] Drama and novel in the fifties might also have had a significant influence in shaping the milieu for the new quest. We only point to *J. B.* by Archibald MacLeish, published in 1957. But it was not until the appearance of Gabriel Vahanian's *The Death of God* in 1961 that the new quest of God manifested itself as a trend of theological reflection.

Our aim here is not to move from a general understanding of God to the more specific Christian understanding. Rather, we wish to show how in Protestant theology today the question of God is raised in a new way and what this implies for the hermeneutical problem. Our own response to the present theological situation is argued through in terms of our understanding of the inner rationale of the Christian faith.[18]

THE NONRELIGIOUS GOD

Bishop Robinson claims that his main problem is his inability to understand God as "up there," as Old Man Upstairs beyond the sky, or as "out there" in a somewhat modified modern fashion. Wherever he turns in nature he finds no space left where God could dwell.

Sharing the general world view of modern man, he faces a dilemma: "To be asked to give up any idea of a Being 'out there' at all will appear to be an outright denial of God. For, to the ordinary way of thinking, to believe in God means to be convinced of the existence of such a supreme and separate Being. 'Theists' are those who believe that such a Being exists, 'atheists' those who deny that he does." [19] Robinson himself still wishes to believe in God, but not in God as *a* being. Instead of thinking of God as *a* being he appeals to ultimate reality: "And one cannot argue whether ultimate reality *exists*. One can only ask what ultimate reality is like. . . . Thus, the fundamental theological question consists not in establishing the 'existence' of God as a separate entity but in pressing through in ultimate concern to what Tillich calls 'the ground of our being.' " [20]

How does one get to know God as the ground of being? Robinson suggests three possibilities. First, by acknowledging the unconditional element in the totality of our experience. Secondly and more supremely so, in probing our relationships with other persons. These are not so much the relationships of religious people as the everyday relationships of men in their depth dimension. Thus Robinson asserts: "To believe in God as love means to believe that in pure personal relationship we encounter, not merely what ought to be, but what is, the deepest, veriest truth about the structure of reality." [21] Finally, knowledge of God is mediated through Jesus Christ: "The Christian's faith is in Christ as the revelation, the laying bare, of the very heart and being of ultimate reality." [22] Knowing God through the totality of our experience, through personal relationships, and through Jesus Christ are certainly three avenues which Robinson wishes us to take seriously. But he is vague on how significant knowledge of God in Jesus Christ really is. Also the knowledge of God through the totality of our experience seems to be dwarfed by what we learn of him in an encounter with other persons. We are told that Jesus Christ persuades us of "the ultimate personal character of reality." When one asks, however, where one can find God in Christ, it appears that Robinson directs us to a personal encounter with the fellowman. Whether or not one knows God depends on how deeply one has loved. The dimension of man's relationship with God appears as the other side of man's relationship with man. This is especially patent in Robinson's view of prayer: "My own experience is that I am really praying for people, agonizing with God for them, precisely *as* I meet them and really give my soul to them." He also speaks of prayer as "the responsibility to meet others with *all* I have, to be ready to encounter the unconditional in the conditional. . . ." To be sure, Robinson knows another side of prayer, a detachment from the engagement with the fellowman. But he would hardly consider it the gist of prayer. What really counts is "sacred secularity," in which a man finds God in the world.[23]

Three problems present themselves in Bishop Robinson's position, the first related to his confidence that God is ultimate reality, the second to his affirmation that what he is presenting is a nonreligious interpretation of God, and the third to his concept of Jesus Christ.

To take the last one first: the difficulty raised by his view of the significance of Jesus Christ for understanding God. He begins with the presupposition that a revolution is in the making which overthrows the belief in a merely "supernatural God." But how crucial is this revolution? Does Robinson understand the revolution already introduced by the event of the incarnation? For Jewish thinking it was revolutionary to affirm that God was incarnate in a man. If Robinson would more carefully think through the revolution introduced by Jesus Christ, he would perhaps also see more clearly the difference between the incarnate love of God and brittle human love. Can the encounter with the fellowman reveal what the cross reveals?

Secondly, Robinson's attempt at a nonreligious interpretation is ambiguous.[24] He wants to speak to the man "for whom the consolations of religion, the *deus ex machina*, the god-hypothesis, are dead beyond recall." [25] Why should this man, however, be interested in the ground of being at all? What concern for the unconditional in personal relationships will he have? The fact is that Robinson does not operate with completely secular categories. In order to speak of the concern of man for God he retains religious terms. Only he does not call them religious.[26]

In "The Debate Continues," the chapter that concludes *The Honest to God Debate*, Robinson responds to the discussion triggered by his book, seeking to clarify its purpose.[27] He says he was not so much concerned with finding the right image of God as with "the detaching of the Christian doctrine of God from any necessary dependence on a 'supernaturalistic' world-view." Christian terms, such as "God," "Christ," and "salvation," are going through a currency crisis, and we must ask ourselves what their cash value still is. We should try to find a new currency, one "that will be convertible in the modern world. And the most distinctive fact about this world is that it is a *secular* world." The so-called secular world is the place where secularization takes place, a process that is neither good nor evil from the perspective of the Christian faith, but simply neutral. Man looks at the world in a new way. What makes modern man truly secular is his loss of the sense of God. "Secularism stands for the conviction that the circle of explanation and control in human affairs can and should be closed—that one does not have to 'bring in God' to account for the weather, or the origins of the universe, or the soul, or the foundations of morality, or anything else." For most practical purposes man "manages" quite happily by himself. We must look for the meaning of God and Christ in the context of the secular view of life. Modern man might appreciate a Christ "who could be Lord of a genuinely secular world, who does not require of them that they become religious first before they can become Christian."

What meaning can there possibly be in these words? Why should men look for a Lord of the secular world if they can manage all right without one? What would they need a Lord for? The secular weather? That they can almost control by themselves. The origins of the universe? Science can give a sufficient account of them. The soul? Psychotherapy can take care of it. Morality? Hollywood is able to give guidance. Anything else?

It would be pointless to assume that all men are religious or consciously live with the god-hypothesis. But would Christ as "Lord of a genuinely secular world" make sense to someone who did not long for a Lord? And is not Christ as Lord merely another way of speaking of a world under God, a world that in its ultimate dimension is theonomous? Who cares for a theonomous world if not one who longs for God? Robinson seems aware of man's need in this respect. But it is on this score that his intention of a non-religious interpretation proves ambiguous.

Understanding Paul van Buren to suggest that "the Christian who takes his secularity seriously can and must abjure metaphysics," Robinson comments: "I cannot share his denigration of natural theology, and I am profoundly convinced of the missionary task of theology to modern man outside the Church, which he seems to deny." [28] Does Robinson see the far-reaching implications of his objection to van Buren as regards his own position? He affirms man's natural awareness of God. In order to describe it he uses religious terms.

As compared with the question of man's natural awareness of God, the problem of the "supernatural God" dwindles in importance. Of all the participants in *The Honest to God Debate* John Macquarrie comes closest to raising the crucial point: "In asking the question of God, man must already have some idea of God, for every question has its direction, and it is impossible to seek anything without having some understanding of what is sought, however vague and minimal that understanding may be." [29] Why should man think of God at all? Why should he show interest in a Lord? It is disconcerting to see how Robinson is trying to suggest that he is presenting a nonreligious God. In the light of the traditional use of the terms, Robinson's language of the "numinous and the ecstatic" can be called nothing but religious. The claim that understanding God "has nothing to do with 'religion'" is special pleading that is not supported by Robinson's own procedure. [30]

Considering the results of the discussion begun by Robinson's book, David L. Edwards, the editor of *The Honest to God Debate*, finds that what "has been achieved so far has been little more than a series of gestures to show that some Christians are anxious to enter into a real conversation with more typical citizens of our secular society." [31] No one would seriously want to object to these conversations. But the conditions for such conversations have to be examined beforehand. Daniel Jenkins writes in *The Honest to God Debate* about the futility of establishing a religionless Christianity: "If we . . . begin to give ourselves airs as the founding members of a new race of 'religionless Christians' we shall quickly find ourselves losing our mature manhood. . . . We shall need to have the 'religious presupposition' established again, to be convicted of sin and led to righteousness." [32] In an age that views itself as thoroughly secular it is beside the point to try to establish again what seems lost: the religious presupposition. But we dare not avoid its critical examination, especially in view of the fact that Robinson himself cannot escape using religious language.

The lack of clarity in the concept of a nonreligious interpretation accounts for the third difficulty of Robinson's position: the quick assertion that ultimate reality is God. He makes it seem plausible that God is: "The word 'God' denotes the ultimate depth of all our being." [33] He sees no special difficulty at this point. What we can ascertain of his hermeneutic in this context is that the "necessity for the name 'God' lies in the fact that our being has depths which naturalism . . . cannot or will not recognize." [34] The hermeneutical difficulty of this view lies in its seemingly uncritical confidence that the depths of man's being are "God."

Robinson's book articulates the initial thrust of the new quest of God. A more radical raising of the hermeneutical question, however, would prevent Robinson from considering the God "up there" or "out there" the foremost stumbling block.[35] Was it not difficult to understand God before the imagery of the universe changed? Although today man must measure the dimensions of the universe differently, the quality of the difficulty of understanding God in the "old" universe might well have been very much the same. It is obvious that the "new" universe involves new problems for theology. But that it should present *the* major difficulty for understanding God is not quite as clear. How is it possible for man to equate the depths of being with God? What drives a man to make this equation? It is this problem that demands the deepening of the quest of God by the hermeneutical concern. To use Macquarrie's terms, what is the understanding, however vague and minimal it may be, that Christian theology presupposes as man's natural awareness of the reality to which the word "God" might refer?

THE GOD OF SPECIAL REVELATION

Helmut Gollwitzer's *The Existence of God as Confessed by Faith,* published in Munich in 1963, the same year as *Honest to God,* is also addressed to the mood that intrigued Bishop Robinson. It is an attempt, however, to show why the kind of position just reviewed is pointless. It objects to demoting God to a word that describes nothing more than an interpersonal experience. The present overview of Gollwitzer's position cannot bring out the subtleties of the argument, the thorough exegetical work and the breadth of the debate with contemporary theology and philosophy. But it might serve as an indication that German theology shares in a new quest of God. It is significant that the English translation of Gollwitzer's book contains in an appendix his review article of *Honest to God,* published in June 1964 in the popular German magazine *Der Spiegel.*[36] Meanwhile Thomas J. J. Altizer, whose work we shall discuss later, has published on this side of the Atlantic a review critical of Gollwitzer's book.[37] A transatlantic discussion on the new quest of God is obviously a reality.

Gollwitzer appeals to a consensus among Continental Protestant theologians as to the demand for a non-objective language about God.[38] In his opinion orthodox as well as existentialist theologians are in agreement on this point. God is not an object among other objects; he makes sense only in relation to man's existence: thus no one can speak of God without appealing to his faith in God. Utterances about God are founded upon the experience of a new life in faith. Gollwitzer realizes that the old alliance between metaphysics and theology has been terminated from both sides. He wonders, however, whether the end of the metaphysical view of the Christian God excludes the further use of such concepts as God's being or God's existence. If they are still being used, does this indicate a continuation of the objectivism of traditional metaphysics?

Gollwitzer develops his approach with reference to the German theologian Herbert Braun, who regards God as no more than the *Whence* of man's being when it is agitated by the encounter with the neighbor. God here becomes an aspect of togetherness or of co-humanity. For Braun God is not the highest being that controls history, but the fulness of a moment of co-humanity. Jesus in this view represents for man the possibility by which he can understand his life as being held or kept from beyond.

The whole tenor of Gollwitzer's argument is based on the idea that biblical thought excludes any kind of objectification. But, says Gollwitzer, the biblical witnesses did not proceed to do what modern theologians are doing. Although they did not speak of an objectifiable givenness of God, they did refer to him as a *Subject* in a rather blunt way. In the Bible, God is the Creator and man is his creature. Both are incomparably different. The ontological difference between Creator and creature has to be affirmed without attempting to develop an ontology of the difference. What men generally think of as God might be completely different from what the Bible says of God. In Plato's and Kant's systems, for example, an action of God has no place. But God is truly God only as the God who acts.

In Gollwitzer's terms the central confrontation with God takes place in Jesus Christ. The man from Nazareth is not the symbol of a generally available relationship between God and man, but God speaking to us. God is not different in his real being from what he is in his Word in Jesus Christ, although one must understand that he is present in Christian language only analogically. And in this instance analogy implies similarity between completely dissimilar things.

Gollwitzer also wishes to speak of God as person. The term for him is a relational concept and does not imply substance. Goethe's aphorism, "What is it to me, your scorn of the All and

One; the professor is a person, but God is none!", presupposes a wrong concept of person. Personal being is being-in-relation, which can be experienced only in the I-Thou dimension. The focus of this dimension is God's encounter with man in Jesus Christ. Thus Christian language about God relates to a confrontation with the man from Nazareth. The Gospel is the determinative factor in our language about God. In the terms of the Gospel, God appears in the vocative. He *is* as "Thou art!" [39] This is the only basis for theological ontology. Jesus Christ is not the fulfillment of a vaguely felt need of man. He is the revelation of the God of whom man was not aware before.

Gollwitzer is convinced that the biblical witnesses understand themselves as instruments of a history of encounter in which someone new confronts us in humanly unsurpassable strangeness. They point to a reality for which man has no built-in possibilities of understanding. There is no common ground between the God of the Christian revelation and what man thinks of God otherwise. God as general anthropological truth, accessible on the basis of man's nature, is not God, but man accessible to himself. We do not know God through creation or a *general* revelation, only through special revelation. Of himself man does not know that he is addressed by God. This he knows only through revelation, a new confrontation with God. God must address man in order that man become involved in a relationship to God and recognize the world as testimony to God. Whenever one receives grace and forgiveness, one receives it from him of whom one knew nothing before. Nietzsche's word that God is dead never pertained to the living God, only to the God of a non-Christian metaphysic.[40]

In Gollwitzer's radical objection to man's awareness of God, the central theological issue for present-day Protestant theology is clearly drawn. The truly radical question is not in what sense God might be "up there" or "out there," but whether or not man has any awareness of God at all. The wrestle with the God "up there" or "out there" is a reaction to a specific time-conditioned interpretation of historical revelation. More basic is the question of how man is able to understand the God of historical revelation.

While Bishop Robinson at least touches upon the hermeneutical question, Gollwitzer discards it. He still proceeds in terms of the Barth-Brunner debate with respect to the point of contact for man's knowledge of God. Even though man might have no natural *knowledge* of God, hermeneutical responsibility requires that the primordial structure of man's experience be carefully examined. What does it mean that man is accessible to himself? What does he find as he seeks to understand himself? Why is man able to posit God as general anthropological truth?

THE GOD OF THE LINGUISTIC BLIK

Paul van Buren's *The Secular Meaning of the Gospel*, another 1963 publication, is the American counterpart to Gollwitzer's radical denial of man's natural knowledge of God. Bishop Robinson, although disagreeing with van Buren's position on this point, has much praise for the book: "A brilliantly original thesis and something of a theological *tour de force*, it seeks to do justice to an orthodox Christology based on Barth and Bonhoeffer at the same time as taking the philosophical critique of Wittgenstein and the linguistic analysts with equal seriousness. I believe it is a major contribution and may already bear out my conviction that in retrospect *Honest to God* 'will be seen to have erred in not being nearly radical enough'." [41]

Van Buren advocates "a reduction of Christian faith to its historical and ethical dimensions." [42] Like Robinson, van Buren presupposes the changed world view. But he is more interested in the *modern Christian* who is also a secular man. He is not at all trying to interpret the faith to the unbeliever. He presupposes that even for the Christian the Christian faith today no longer makes sense in the context of the language of religion and asks whether there still are language dimensions in which the Christian faith can become meaningful.

According to van Buren, Christians have a certain "blik," which means that they look at life on the basis of their commitment to Christ. A "natural sense of the divine . . . natural religion and a natural revelation" do not contribute anything to an understanding of God. All that we can say about God is how we use the word "God" in our language: "The language of Christian faith is the language of a believer, one who has been 'caught' by the Gospel. Insofar as his 'blik' is functioning, his language is the language of faith, whether he is speaking about some generally recognized religious subject, such as 'God,' or of some so-called secular subject, like politics or his job. The function of his words may be to enlighten his listener concerning his 'blik.' In other circumstances they may take the form of an invitation to share that 'blik.' . . . The actual function of the words is the key to understanding the language of faith." [43]

No specific referent is available for the word "God." Today we no longer believe that God lives in a tree and that he might die if the tree burned down.[44] There comes a point where we begin to wonder whether the word "God" refers to anything at all. On this score believers owe themselves and others clarity: "If 'God' is not a word which refers to something, they should be careful not to use it in a way that suggests that it does." All that believers can say when they use the word "God" is that it refers to a certain "blik": "If they are talking about a 'blik,' rather than about 'how things are,' they should say so." [45]

The way this works out theologically is that van Buren turns to Jesus Christ, viewing him in terms of the historical perspective. Whatever van Buren says about God is related to the Gospel which declares that "in the history of Jesus of Nazareth something universal, eternal, absolute, something it calls 'God,' was manifested." [46] All I can find in van Buren as interpretation of the word "God" is that in the man Jesus a claim of love has been experienced. The word "God" here has become the title of the experience of the Gospel or of the encounter with Jesus. The believer ascribes a certain value to this particular event. He values it as God.

The historical event has the character of the transcendent. Faith does not originate in itself, but is a reaction to the history of Jesus: "The language of faith, by referring to a transcendent element, indicates that something has happened to the believer, rather than that he has done something." [47] The use of the words tells van Buren that God as transcendent reality actually implies

a reference to the transcendence of history, specifically one historical event. God is experienced in this dimension only. The ab-
soluteness of this singular event is God.

In a footnote which marks the end of the book, van Buren
casts an interesting light on the relationship between his effort
and that of Bishop Robinson. He repeats his basic conviction that
we are entering a time in which the Christian must discover what
he calls the secular meaning of the Gospel: "Bishop Robinson
agrees with me that this discovery depends upon a radical recon-
sideration of theological method. . . . Had Bishop Robinson re-
versed the order of his chapters on 'The Ground of Being' and
'The Man for Others,' and reflected more on the language involved in both areas, our conclusions would have been even more
similar than they are." [48]

It is difficult to see what might be gained for a radically new
understanding of theological method by reversing the order between theology and Christology.[49] Hermeneutically, Robinson's
approach is to be preferred, since he still presupposes God as a
referent that is significant in itself. His probing of the depth dimension of human life shows that he is still aware of an ontological dimension in man's experience. The reversal of Robinson's
order between theology and Christology would entail the loss of
the ontological dimension.

What is methodologically remarkable in van Buren's position
is not that he moves from Christology to theology or, rather, that
he absorbs theology in Christology, but that he begins with a prior
understanding of both which unquestioningly accepts the secular
interpretation of modern life. The word "God" is dead for van
Buren because all that modern man still knows as ultimate referent
is the world. He prejudges his case from the outset insofar as he
does not admit any other dimension except the language of so-
called secular man, which excludes any meaning other than the
one implied in his secular frame of mind. If nothing is left in
man's experience as an ultimate but the world, the Gospel itself
must be reduced to a secular phenomenon.[50] That is the simple
logic of it all.[51]

But does van Buren's ontological presupposition—that the
secular is the ultimate—allow him to give a true account of the

human condition? Is he not absolutizing a particular interpretation of contemporary existence? [52] Is it really true that the actual function of words as they are used today knows only of the historical and ethical dimensions of human existence?

THE DEAD GOD

Van Buren differs from Robinson and Gollwitzer in denying God as distinct referent. His stance is often identified with what William Hamilton in an uncommonly evocative essay has described as "The Death of God Theology." [53] Hamilton's article is crucial to understanding the new quest of God.[54] He makes us aware of important differences between the English and American points of view: "The British publication of Bishop Robinson's *Honest to God* partly created and partly released forces that may well be coming together into a new theological movement in that country. And there is an American counterpart to this British movement, though it goes back in time a bit before *Honest to God.* I am going to call this American movement the death of God theology."

Hamilton believes that the American death of God theology is more radical than the British "radical theology" represented by Bishop Robinson: "To the death of God theologian, Robinson is far too confident about the possibility of God-language. To use Paul van Buren's terms, Robinson is perfectly right to reject objectified theism, but he is wrong to think that his non-objectified theism is any more satisfactory." After having voiced his disagreement with British radical theology, Hamilton turns to outlining the American death of God tradition in theology and to linking it to the present American theological debate as a whole.[55]

While neoorthodoxy claimed that, although man could not know God, God had made himself known to man, the death of God theology asserts that God does not make himself known. Hamilton is emphatic in stressing the newness of the approach he represents: "This is more than . . . the usual assurance that before the holy God all our language gets broken and diffracted into paradox. It is really that we do not know, do not adore, do not possess, do not believe in God. It is not just that a capacity has dried up within us; we do not take all this as merely a statement about our frail psyches, we take it as a statement about the nature of the world and we try to convince others. God is dead. We are not talking about the absence of the experience of God, but about the experience of the absence of God." One wonders why the experience of the absence of God must be called the death of God. Apparently Hamilton knows no other word for it.

In order to make his point, Hamilton refers in particular to two 1963 publications, Thomas Altizer's *Mircea Eliade and the Dialectic of the Sacred* and Paul van Buren's *The Secular Meaning of the Gospel*. Altizer's vision "beginning with man accepting, affirming, even willing the death of God in a radical sense, ends with man willing to . . . undergo the discipline of darkness, the dark night of the soul . . . while the possibility of a new epiphany of the sacred, a rebirth of the possibility of having God once more is awaited." Van Buren is determined by linguistic analysis and believes "that analytical philosophy has made all language about God impossible."

While Altizer is influenced by the cosmic dimension of the disappearance of the sacred and van Buren by secular language, Hamilton turns to a new interpretation of the Reformation. As over against the late nineteenth century, which saw the major significance of the Reformation in the autonomous religious personality, and the first half of the twentieth century, which discovered in the Reformation the righteous God, Hamilton underlines the move away from the cloister to the world: "I am starting with a definition of Protestantism as a movement away from the sacred place." The effect of the movement away from God and religion "is the more important movement into, for, towards the world, worldly life, and the neighbor as the bearer of the worldly Jesus."

Hamilton substitutes for his loss of God obedience to Jesus. But it is obedience to the *worldly* Jesus! Instead of looking for Jesus in the Scriptures he seeks him in the neighbor, in the struggle for justice and order. Jesus is masked in the world. The task of the Christian is to tear off the masks and to work together with him in the world. The move into the world also demands a turning toward the self, "a look within in order to become Jesus." When we have an experience of the absence of God, nothing is left to turn to but world and self; here only can the motives of Christian action be found: "We are not proceeding from God and faith to neighbor and love, loving in such and such a way because we are loved in such and such a way. We move to our neighbor, to the city and to the world out of a sense of the loss of God."

There are two major problems in this position. First, what does it mean to make decisions in the city or the world together with Jesus or in becoming Jesus? For Hamilton, Protestant theology "belongs in the street. . . . The academy and the temple can, for now, no longer be trusted as theological guides." But one wonders *how* one should act in the street relative to "power, culture, art, sex, money, the Jew, the Negro, beauty, ugliness, poverty and indifference," the areas which Hamilton specifies. Does one simply act and then discover Jesus by unmasking him in the world or in oneself? Hamilton certainly would not wish to suggest that *any* type of action in the street is desirable, just so there is action. Since he refers so much to Jesus, would it not be proper to ask what type of action Jesus was involved in in the street? Did not the church remember Jesus to have said that the law of his being was to do the will of his Father in heaven? Was not the point of his action to show the relevance of the character and being of God to the street as well as to the temple? It seems somewhat too easy to claim that one acts together with Jesus in the street or that one becomes Jesus without examining the context of Jesus' thought and action.

The other problem in Hamilton relates to his emphasis on love of neighbor and enemy. Why should it be so important to be concerned about the world, culture, sex, money, the Jew, the Negro, etc.? Why be an integrationist rather than a segregationist? Does love of neighbor come naturally? Langdon Gilkey sees the difficulty involved when he says that "a sense of this claim of love upon us has been no more certain and surely no more universal than has been the certainty of a divine or holy dimension in reality." [56] Is love of neighbor an end in itself? Why should I love my neighbor rather than be indifferent to him? Might not love of neighbor, without being grounded in the mandate of an ultimate reality, be mere fancy? The loss of the sense of God might as easily paralyze my love of neighbor as activate it. Before admitting too quickly to an experience of the absence of God, one would wish to know whether the problem has been adequately defined. Hamilton regards religion as "any system of thought or action in which God or the gods serve as fulfiller of needs or solver of problems." [57] If the reality of God, by definition, is tied to the religious *a priori* in this sense, it is obvious that there is a loss of the sense of God today. But is it not possible that the God factor enters the mind of at least some men for reasons other than need-fulfillment or problem-solving? Is it not an evasive statement of the problem if one speaks of God as though he had always been understood only as need-fulfiller and problem-solver?

The central hermeneutical formulation of Hamilton refers to the breakdown of the religious *a priori* which "means that there is no way, ontological, cultural, or psychological, to locate a part of the self or a part of human experience that needs God. There is no God-shaped blank within man. Man's heart may or may not be restless until it rests in God. It is not necessarily so. God is not in the realm of the necessary at all; he is not necessary being. . . . " [58] The argument on Hamilton's premises would make more sense if he would stop at this point. But he goes on to speak of a waiting for God, the possibility that God might still play a role, but different from that of need-fulfiller and problem-solver. If God is dead, why wait for him? And if we should wait for him, how should we *understand* him when he returns? It might have been necessary at this point to distinguish between the biblical God and the God-idea of Western culture. Are we to wait for the return of the God of the God-idea or for the God who is the Father of our Lord Jesus Christ? Or is there no difference between the two?

I believe Hamilton's position is evidence for the need of joining the new quest of God to the hermeneutical concern. Hamilton, too, cannot avoid the issue of understanding. And it would move the debate on were he to examine his hermeneutical rationale more thoroughly. He says: "If God is not needed, if it is to the world and not God that we repair for our needs and problems, then perhaps we may come to see that He is to be enjoyed and delighted in. Part of the meaning of waiting for God is found in this attempt to understand what delighting in Him might mean." To *understand* what delighting in him might *mean?* What is the structure of man's understanding? What are its elements? The debate about the death of God has not as yet arrived at its primal level. Hamilton has not examined his tacit assumption that man might be able to *understand* what delighting in God might mean.

Hamilton believes that our "ethical existence is partly . . . an actual Christology." Does he ever get beyond a *Jesus*ology? And why should one be interested in Jesus? The forces that are joining in declaring that God is dead have no reason to be more interested in the values centered in Jesus. The history of the church could teach us that the dead God soon is followed by the dead Christ. And after the dead Christ? Nothing?

Hamilton wishes to relate what he considers the American death of God tradition in theology to "the very lively theological discussion going on right now in this country." The discussion covers a wide range. We will consider two other theologies in addition to that of van Buren. The first is an attempt to establish a more philosophical theology, the second an effort to opt for a more kerygmatic approach.

THE NATURAL GOD

A *Christian Natural Theology*, by John B. Cobb, Jr., is a programmatic attempt to reintroduce philosophical theology with the help of Alfred North Whitehead's philosophy. The book is perhaps the outstanding 1965 American publication in the field of systematic theology. Cobb seeks to recast theology in a framework in which God can again be a serious referent.

In Cobb's perspective the death of God theology with its reductionism is self-defeating: "Those who believe that the gospel requires no reference to God in any sense other than a special mode of human existence or togetherness seem to me not to have realized that the same cultural and intellectual forces that have militated against the meaningfulness of the word 'God' operate also against most of that which they continue to affirm." Cobb confesses that he cannot think theologically apart from God as a referent: "Indeed for my own spiritual existence as a Christian it is a matter of life and death that the reality of the referent of 'God' be a part of my intellectual conviction." [59] On the basis of Whitehead's thought Cobb proceeds to show how the reality of God is still intellectually acceptable.

It is unnecessary for our purposes to restate the complex argument of Cobb as he reintroduces Whitehead's view of God. The sum of Whitehead's position—as interpreted by Cobb—is that God is "an actual entity who envisages and orders the realm of eternal possibilities. He adds himself to the world as the vision of ideal possibility, from which every new occasion takes its rise, thereby ensuring a measure of order and value in a situation that could otherwise be only chaotic and indeed could achieve no actuality at all. The world, in its turn, reacts upon him so as to affect the way in which he, in his turn, acts upon it." [60] Logically Whitehead's argument for the existence of God grows out of an intuition, according to Cobb: "There is a deep human intuition that the order of the world requires for its explanation some principle of order that cannot entirely be attributed to the entities that constitute the world." The proof for God's existence is supposed to be quite obvious: "That there *is* something which we may properly call God is sufficiently indicated by the kind of order that is visible to all." [61]

It might have strengthened Cobb's position considerably had he approached his argument from the hermeneutical perspective of systematic theology. How does the question of God arise at all in the Christian faith? Cobb almost immediately confronts us with Whitehead's thought and only toward the end of the book asks what the philosophical scheme of Whitehead might contribute to understanding the great religious intuitions of mankind: "The adequacy of a philosophical scheme must be tested against these intuitions just as much as against the findings of the natural sciences." [62] It is a moot question, however, whether the theologian *can begin* methodologically where the philosopher begins, regardless of whether his name is Whitehead or not.[63]

What actually goes on when the Christian, following one great religious intuition of mankind, refers to God in Christ? Is it really the case that the Christian presupposes knowledge of the *order* of the universe which suggests to him that "there *is* something which we may properly call God?" [64] I do not object to the broad definition of theology given by Cobb: "One's work is theology even if one ignores all earlier statements and begins only with the way things appear to him from that perspective which he acknowledges as given to him in some community of shared life and conviction." [65] But I do not discover in Cobb a description of how the question of God hermeneutically develops in the community of shared life and conviction in which the Christian finds himself. What is the question of the Christian community which Cobb is trying to answer? In the face of the present dissolution of theology, one should not fail to be more explicit as regards the specific hermeneutical problem of the Christian community if one —like Cobb—wishes to save God as the referent of Christian theology. From our perspective Cobb philosophically tries to state too much without having carefully articulated the primary hermeneutical quest.

THE GOD OF MYSTERY

William Hordern's *Speaking of God: The Nature and Purpose of Theological Language*, a 1964 publication written in the vein of kerygmatic theology, develops the hermeneutical issue of the Christian experience of God with considerable acumen, even though Hordern does not use the word "hermeneutical." The book as a whole is an attempt to open up a conversation between theology and analytical philosophy. The first half of the book is largely a history of this type of philosophy. It also introduces the reader to the nature of a language game à la Wittgenstein. Theology is defined as a specific language game that articulates Christian convictions.

How does the Christian understand God? He lives "in a community bound together by a common faith." In this community language about God "points to a convictor who is known to be a mystery." God is basically a mystery. It is important to note that Hordern at this point refers to Bishop Robinson's struggle with the God "up there" and "out there": "We must see that terms like 'up there' were never used in Christian terminology to locate God in space. . . . In speaking of God as 'high and lifted up' Christians have confessed the mystery of God." To Hordern "a mystery is not unknown but unknowable." With the increase of our knowledge the mystery increases rather than decreases.[66]

How does the sense of mystery arise? Man faced with existence and the universe is led to ask the question: Why is there something and not nothing? Actually it is not a question at all: "It does not formulate any problem about the unknown for which we could seek a solution by making something known. But it does express a sense of awe, wonder, and reverence before the mystery of existence." The sense of mystery is universal, although it does not prove God's existence: "It is compatible with many views of God, and even the atheist may be aware of the mystery of the universe. Mystery does not prove God's existence, but it helps us to understand the use of theological language." God is known only in the community of faith. For it is here that "God, the Mystery, has revealed himself." [67]

The mystery is experienced by believers and unbelievers alike. The unbeliever does not know, however, that he is experiencing God in his sense of mystery. Only when he begins to believe in the revealed God does he know. But apart from experiencing the *mystery* there can be no understanding of God: "Without the experience of mystery the meaning of the word 'God' is distorted." [68] What Hordern apparently wants to say is that in the experience of mystery man has a pre-awareness of God, so that he is able to understand him when he reveals himself.

Is it necessary, however, to appeal to the concept of mystery as a hermeneutical presupposition for understanding God? Hordern introduces a second hermeneutical argument which is less involved and which might be quite sufficient to come to grips with the actual hermeneutical situation. On the final pages of the book he refers to Paul Tillich: "Every man, believes Tillich, has to be an ontologist, for man is aware that he consists of both being and nonbeing. Since nonbeing threatens being, man longs to find the power of being that can save him from nonbeing." Everything participates in being. "To say that 'God is' is to make a dramatic statement about the nature of reality, it is ontological." [69] But instead of asking what is involved in the fact that the Christian speaks ontologically of God, Hordern stresses the need for a specific Christian ontology: "The Christian faith stands or falls with certain specific statements about reality—'God was in Christ,' 'God is love.' Insofar as Christianity makes such statements it is committed implicitly to certain ontological affirmations. . . . In this case, far from being indifferent to ontology, Christianity has its own ontology to offer." [70] Here Hordern skips the primal hermeneutical step: he does not fully articulate the general ontological element contained in Christian theology. It must be made explicit that the affirmation "God is love" is an utterance that contains a general declaration about being insofar as the word "is" is used. Hordern sees that understanding goes beyond a mere knowledge of language: "As Wittgenstein points out, if we are in a strange country, with entirely strange traditions, we may master the language but still we do not *'understand* the people.' " [71] But Hordern does not explicate what is *hermeneutically* involved in the claim of the Gospel that its affirmation about God as love is *true.* That Christianity is not merely a language game but a truth claim is something that one does not learn in Hordern.

Hordern gets as close to the hermeneutical mandate of the new quest of God as any one of the authors reviewed. But he also illustrates that the new quest of God could profit from a fuller articulation of the hermeneutical problem. The nuclear structure of man's quest of God needs more specific clarification than Hordern offers. The hermeneutical question must be raised as a specific theme.

THE HERMENEUTICAL PRESUPPOSITION

The present discussion directs us to fundamentals. Interest in the lofty systematic structures is dwindling. The battle of presuppositions has been joined. Robinson, Gollwitzer, van Buren, Hamilton, Cobb and Hordern represent a trend in England, Germany and the United States that is turning to a reexamination of theological prejudgments.[72] Bishop Robinson's comment is characteristic in this respect: "I was questioning one whole set of presuppositions and feeling towards another in its place." [73]

We indicated before that in our opinion it would be pointless to reintroduce the religious presupposition as countermeasure to Bishop Robinson's proposals. Nevertheless, we must inquire what ontological presupposition religion might imply.[74] Religion might be a primitive way of expressing an inescapable experience. Even though modern man apparently is not religious, he might still have to react to the same fundamental ontological structure that expressed itself in ancient and medieval man as religion.

Hermeneutically it would be misleading, however, to define man's elementary ontological awareness immediately in religious terms. Langdon Gilkey hopes that the religious character of man can become revealed again: the fact that man is related to an ultimate beyond himself. With this as starting point he tries to develop a new theology.[75] But he can take this avenue only because he relegates the hermeneutical question to a secondary position. Whether men sense the numinous is not what immediately matters for theological hermeneutic. The hermeneutical starting point for theology is the simple phenomenon that the theologian says— together with the church—"God is." For Robinson God *is* as ultimate reality, for Gollwitzer as Thou, for Cobb as ultimate order, for Hordern as mystery. Those who wait for God, like Hamilton, wait for him as one who "is to be." The point to be made here as regards every theological effort has been well summarized by Karl Barth with respect to dogmatic theology: "Dogmatics, in each and all of its divisions and subdivisions, with every one of its questions and answers, with all its biblical and historical assertions, with the whole range of its formal and material considerations, examinations and condensations, can first and last, as a whole and in part, say nothing but that God is." [76] At the nucleus of the hermeneutical problem of theology lies the question: What does the word "is" imply when predicated of God?

Besides sensing himself and the world, man senses being. This is not an irrational experience. It *antecedes* man's reasoning. It is best described as prerational or precognitive, a primordial "urge," a "sixth sense," as it were. It is not a by-product of man's cognitive relationship to society or nature. It is not the result of his reflections on *a* supreme being. It is an immediate awareness transcending any encounter with nature or other human beings. It also transcends the historical and ethical dimensions of human life.[77]

An appeal to man's awareness of being is by no means an attempt to reintroduce the proofs for God's existence. Recently Schubert M. Ogden has suggested that on account of Charles Hartshorne's work "the question of the nature and place of the arguments for God's existence has once again become an open one for Protestant theology." Hartshorne does not want to infer God from something that is not God. All proofs for God's existence, Ogden quotes Hartshorne as saying, "depend upon conceptions which derive their meaning from God himself. They are merely ways of making clear that we already and once for all believe in God, though not always with clearness and consistency." [78] Perhaps there are some recent philosophers, Hartshorne among them, who take God into account in their respective systems. The theologian appealing to them might receive some help in proving to himself the reasonableness of what he assumes. Hermeneutically, however, he has to press beyond the idea of God or a knowledge of God so-called. The attempt to prove God's existence admittedly proves no more than that the man who seeks to prove God already *knows* God.[79] But man's understanding of God does not begin on the level of knowledge. Man does not come to understand God by inductive or deductive reasoning. A knowledge of God so-called, whatever its contents may be, is already a reasoned articulation and lies beyond the prior awareness of being.[80] The first hermeneutical step is the examination of this awareness.[81]

Theological hermeneutic dare not even presuppose that the awareness is the *question of God*. Tillich observes that the arguments for the existence of God "are expressions of the *question* of God which is implied in human finitude. This question is their truth; every answer they give is untrue." [82] While Tillich is wrestling with the same phenomenon we are describing, hermeneutically the ontological presupposition of theology is not immediately to be described as the question of God. For some people the ontological awareness may lead to the question of

God, for others not. Tillich goes on to give an even more precise statement of his view: "The question of God is possible because an awareness of God is present in the question of God. This awareness precedes the question. It is not the result of the argument but its presupposition." [83] Tillich too quickly names man's basic ontological awareness "God." The word "God," however, already presupposes a reasoning about an experience. Tillich skips the primary hermeneutical dilemma, man's hermeneutical aporia as regards God, that is, man's puzzlement about his inability to come to grips with the reality of being that he senses.

Tillich stands in the tradition of Schleiermacher, who partly argued from the totality of the world to its Whence, its source or absolute cause. To this Whence man supposedly stands in a relationship of absolute dependence. Man is thus characterized primarily by his createdness. Man's feeling of absolute dependence is here the result of a type of reasoning from a known to an unknown factor. But man's awareness of being is an immediate response to a call without reflection on dependence or independence. Although Schleiermacher's ontological analysis is not without a point, it is a completely gratuitous assumption that man's awareness of being is an awareness of God.

We are describing man's awareness of being as a primordial ontological experience and not as the result of a logical argument from the finite to the infinite. It reflects an immediate encounter with Being beyond our own being and the being of the world. Being beyond our own being evokes an awareness. However, man does not immediately *know* what he senses. It is exactly at this point that the hermeneutical problem begins for theology. Theological hermeneutic must stress that the immediate experience is not instantly known as God. Man is puzzled by his primordial experience. An immediate name is not available. We do not mean this, however, in the sense of *Faust:* "I have no name to give it! Feeling is all in all." We are not thinking of an *ersatz* religion. We are trying to point to the aporia that lies at the basis of all religious experience.

Rudolf Otto lodged a crucial objection against Schleiermacher's reasoning from the feeling of createdness to a cause beyond man that triggers the feeling. According to Otto the feeling of createdness is subject to a more fundamental datum of experience: the awareness of reality beyond oneself and the world: "This 'feeling of reality' . . . must be posited as a primary immediate datum of consciousness, and the 'feeling of dependence' is then a consequence." [84] Man's sense of being is not a derivative of any type of reasoning. Obviously Otto is speaking of it in terms of the religious experience of the wholly Other, the numinous. We wish to appeal only to its ontological aspect or dimension, to that experience which underlies the religious experience.

We cannot strongly enough stress that it is not a cognitive structure which drives man to the awareness of being. In an immediate sense man encounters a reality not commensurate with himself. Man, as it were, is "self-dual." There is always another pole of his being that gives him a sense of primordial communion. Self-duality is not something subconscious or unconscious. Man is aware of it. It belongs to man's self-consciousness. But it is not something objective or cognitive. It is immediate.[85] It is not experienced as ecstasy. Man is aware of it while abiding in himself.

Man's awareness of being, however, is ambiguous. He experiences the urge to "unveil existence" (Feuerbach), to stand in openness before himself. But can he come to grips with this urge? Does his immediate sense of being instantly make sense to him? In responding to the call of being, is man unveiling existence or concealing it? We recall the words of Saul Bellow in the motto of this chapter: "*I look at myself and see chest, thighs, feet—a head. This strange organization, I know it will die. And inside —something, something, happiness . . . 'Thou movest me.' . . . Is it an idiot joy that makes this animal, the most peculiar animal of all, exclaim something?*" [86] The primordial exclamation seeks to break into the cognitive realm. But man is puzzled in trying to articulate his primal experience because he realizes that he is not transparent to himself. He begins to wonder whether he is not deceiving himself when he hears the call of being. Is it an idiot joy that makes man exclaim something? Why "praise" even in Bertolt Brecht's *Grand Chorale of Thanksgiving?*

Praise ye the night and the darkness which surround you!
Gather in crowds,
Look into the heavens above you,
Already the day fleeth from you.

Praise ye the grass and the beast which neighbor you,
        living and dying.
Behold, like to yours
Is the life of the grass and the beast,
Like to yours must be their dying.

Praise ye the tree which groweth exultant from carrion unto
        heaven!
Praise ye carrion,
Praise ye the tree that ate of it
But praise ye the heavens likewise.

Praise ye from your hearts the unmindfulness of heaven!
Since it knoweth not
Either your name or your face,
No one knoweth if you are still there.

Praise ye the cold, the darkness and corruption!
Look beyond:
It heedeth you not one jot.
Unmoved, you may do your dying.[87]

Why exclaim something? Why praise? What is it that is experienced in the awareness of being? Nothing? [88] The hermeneutical presupposition of theology is not a clear-cut awareness. It is an aporia.

THE ONTOLOGICAL APORIA

As stated before, nothing will be gained for the understanding of God by an appeal to some residual religiousness that might still be discovered in modern man.[89] Heidegger, for example, suggests that the phrase "God is dead" says anything but "there is no God." What died was the Absolute.[90] It is quite possible that a case could be made for residual God-yearning in even the most representative "moderns." But it would only distract from the central issue. Hermeneutic compels us to ask why theology claims that God *is*. What is involved in the "is"? Is there a primal word that can give meaning to being?

The theologian is tempted immediately to identify being with God. Tillich, for example, claims: "God is being—itself." [91] All we can state with certainty as regards being, however, is that man has an awareness of being. The "is" in the claim that God *is* refers to this awareness. But the claim must not overlook the fact that man does not know what being means. Theology must pursue its work with the clear understanding that man is caught in an ontological aporia.

The lack of an articulation of this aporia is still noticeable down to the most recent constructive statements of systematic theology. Wolfhart Pannenberg in his outlines of Christology claims that man cannot stop asking for God and thus also thinking the God-idea, whatever the specific word for the idea might be.[92] This does not mean that one already knows God. The God-idea is only a question.

Pannenberg has explicated the question of God more fully in a 1965 essay, "Die Frage nach Gott." Referring to the controversy between Gollwitzer and Braun, he feels that theology has been pressed into a dilemma by the atheistic critique of theism. Either theology claims a special status for its God-talk as in Gollwitzer and yet cannot help that its view of God is confused with that of theism, or the atheistic critique of theism is also extended to Christian God-talk as in Braun.[93]

Pannenberg wishes to relate Christian God-talk to man's experience: revelation uncovers in man the truth to which it refers. He finds in early dialectical theology God-talk that is more related to man's situation than that of Gollwitzer. It is this type of God-talk that he is trying to retain. There is a ground of man's being that sustains man, a power that embraces all reality, man's existence included. Man himself is a question. As he raises the question of the meaning and destiny of his life, he reflects on the question of his existence as a whole as it relates to the nature of the reality that sustains him. The phenomenology of religion suggests to Pannenberg that the power which man sees involved in answering his question has personal character, which is the real reason that makes it possible to interpret the question of human existence as the question of God.

Pannenberg is still committed to the Christian question-answer scheme: man raises a question; theology knows the answer. The question, however, can be raised in a number of ways and may not necessarily be the question of God. Perhaps some men still ask the question of God. But others may merely want to know about being. Whatever question contemporary man might be asking, however, it is hardly possible for him to avoid the ontological aporia: Why is there something and not nothing? Why must I be?

It is understandable that in view of this question a number of theologians appeal to philosophy, especially to Martin Heidegger, for a clarification of man's awareness of being. Heidegger tries to establish an order of priorities for the understanding of God: "Only from the truth of being can the essence of the holy be thought. Only from the essence of the holy is the essence of deity to be thought. Only in the light of the essence of deity can that be thought and said which the word 'God' should name." [94] But Heidegger has difficulties in offering us a *word* that could articulate the truth of being and give it meaning.[95] He is seeking for a language that grows out of the Word—as he understands it. This is part of a vigorous attempt to arrive at a thinking that overcomes the ontological aporia, a thinking no longer burdened by what he calls "the forgetfulness of being." [96] It is a thinking that from the very outset tries to leave behind the realm of the ontological in order to find a home in "being" itself. There comes a point, however, for Heidegger where the word breaks into pieces, as it were. Where "being" is, the articulate word returns to the inarticulate.[97]

Heidegger's own interpretation of language erects a roadblock on the way from the truth of being (via the essence of the holy and the essence of deity) to the word "God." [98] There is a difference between his understanding of the Word and the Christian understanding. For the Christian faith the Word does not disappear in "being." Word and God are coequal primal realities and are not subordinate to "being."

Can man of his own accord ever get beyond the struggle with the truth of being? Man seems to possess the vessel of truth without knowing how to fill it. Gerhard Ebeling has clearly described this dilemma: "The condition on which it is possible to understand what the word 'God' means is a lack of understanding. Of course we must not stop at merely penultimate and provisional lack of understanding. . . . Rather it is a case of experiencing a radical and comprehensive lack of understanding." [99]

Ebeling's point may seem rather abstract. It is made more concrete in a recent film, *The Pawnbroker*, in which the main figure ends up leaning against the wall of a house on a cruel street of New York with no answers whatsoever to his questions.[100] In fact, fate has given him such a beating that he has hardly any questions left to ask. What is left is the radical questionableness of his being. He had been an inmate of a concentration camp in World War II. Having lost wife and children, he comes to the United States where he operates a pawnshop in Harlem. He has isolated himself completely from human intercourse. There no longer seems any point to his life. The past has made him a corpse among the living. But he continues to *be*. It is this hanging on to being in the face of its radical questionableness which provides theology with the primal level for understanding the word "God." Man's understanding of God presupposes a complete lack of understanding.

THE LIMITATION
OF THE HISTORICAL VIEW OF JESUS

*A young man, adamant in his committed life. The one
who was nearest to him relates how, on the last evening, he
arose from supper, laid aside his garments, and washed the
feet of his friends and disciples—an adamant young man,
alone as he confronted his final destiny. . . .*

*He had assented to a possibility in his being, of which
he had had his first inkling when he returned from the des-
ert. If God required anything of him, he would not fail.
Only recently, he thought, had he begun to see more clearly,
and to realize that the road of possibility might lead to the
Cross. . . . The end might be a death without significance
—as well as being the end of the road of possibility.*[1]

DAG HAMMARSKJÖLD

THE overview of the new quest of God showed us that theology
dare not quickly identify the ontological dimension of man's
primal experience with God. But theology cannot act as though
the dimension did not exist. Carefully observing the human condition, theology will note that man on the primal level of his
being is trying to come to grips with the ontological aporia.

In theology concern for man's primal experience can never
be completely dissociated from the historical concern related to
Jesus of Nazareth. Trying to speak to man's ontological aporia,
theology turns to the originating event of the Christian faith. In
many instances theology might not have made the ontological
aporia an explicit theme of its work. But it can never escape
turning to the Christ event. For example, Bishop Robinson speaks

of Christ as the revelation of the very heart of reality. Gollwitzer claims that the true God speaks to us only in Jesus Christ. Van Buren believes that the history of Jesus Christ is the place where the word "God" is illuminated. In these men the historical concern for Jesus Christ is limited to the bare essentials. This is quite understandable in the present situation. The hermeneutical drive in present-day theology is concerned with the elementary components of understanding. Nevertheless, the difficulty in the turn to the historical base of the Christian faith in Jesus of Nazareth is often not fully grasped. In what way can Jesus' history become important for the Christian faith?

We stated before that Protestant theology within the last two decades moved from the demythologizing debate via a new quest of the historical Jesus to a new quest of God, and that the present concern, rather than implying a neglect of the two others, makes both appear in a new light—which is becoming especially important for the new quest of the historical Jesus. Albert Schweitzer could still say that the quest of the historical Jesus was an attempt to come to terms with ancient christological dogma.[2] In more recent years, however, it has become an attempt to come to grips with the man Jesus, especially his relationship to God.[3] While the first half of the twentieth century saw a decline of the quest and a restatement of ancient christological formulas, the last decade has reopened some of the unanswered issues. Regardless of how these issues are tackled, we have to ask in terms of principle how much we can ever hope to accomplish by turning to the origins of the Christian faith in Jesus of Nazareth.

Why is the figure of Jesus important for the Christian faith? It is impossible to attempt an answer without considering the theological debate based on the application of the historico-critical method to Jesus research. The careful reexamination of this method since the early twenties has made it increasingly clear that scholarly research in Jesus' life is always a questing *under the guidance of a specific question.*[4] The old quest was enamored with the concept of historical objectivity and sought to describe Jesus' life in a historico-causal scheme. The new quest is guided by the lodestar of existential understanding and seeks to uncover Jesus' selfhood. The question that guides the new quest has been formulated by James M. Robinson: "A serious quest of the historical Jesus must have meaning in terms of man's quest for meaningful existence." [5] In order to answer its question the new quest employs a complex methodology, a combination of objective historico-critical research and the existential view of history. It tries to unite concern for history as interpretation and concern for history as fact. But it might consider that the application of both historical methods to the origins of Christianity have occasionally made it appear as though there were no radically theological question left to ask. While we cannot neglect historical research, we dare not overlook the inevitability of the theological question. It seems a remnant of the exclusively historical view of Christian origins that today in the new quest of the historical Jesus the question of God has not yet become the central theme.

JESUS AS INTERPRETATION

Form criticism introduced the first modification of the objective historico-causal approach to Jesus' life. The method of the new quest grew out of this modification, which sharply confronted theological scholarship with the difference between Jesus and the theology of the primitive church. Rudolf Bultmann, the outstanding representative of present-day form criticism, is convinced that the New Testament tradition primarily confronts us with the faith of the early Christians and not with Jesus' own words and deeds. We are not dealing exclusively with the early faith community, however, but with the figure of the historical Jesus which emerges through it.[6]

Bultmann begins with the obvious observation that the primitive church did not start out with ready-made Gospels. The oral tradition that was transmitted took shape in accord with the spiritual needs of the church, especially the needs of worship. The basic historical factor for assessing the historicity of the Gospels is the assumption that in the Hellenistic world the proclamation of the Gospel centered in Jesus' death and resurrection. Jesus' words and deeds were recorded in keeping with a basic pattern formed by these two concepts. Originally the resurrection was regarded as the moment when Jesus became the Messiah. But then a change took place: "Gradually . . . his earthly life came to be viewed as the life and work of the Messiah—at first with the reservation, that his Messiahship remained a secret during this period. Hence there lies over the account of Mark the veil of the Messianic secret." [7]

The words and the public ministry of Jesus must be mainly understood as interpretation. Perhaps after careful examination we might still be able to arrive at a historical core of the words. But to look for that which is factually historical means to have a concern different from the Gospels. They are not directly interested in recounting historical detail: "In John the original meaning of the gospel comes out in fullest clarity, in that the evangelist while making free use of the tradition creates the figure of Jesus entirely from faith." [8]

In Bultmann's view Jesus' life is not of central theological concern. It is a *fact* for him that Jesus existed. But we can understand why this fact is important only if we consider that its interpretation by the primitive church centered in cross and resurrection. Although the stress on cross and resurrection establishes an important historical point, as long as the question of God is not raised it is doubtful whether one has been confronted with their most radical significance. I realize that Bultmann raises the question of God in his work as a whole. But it is usually deflected in deference to the role the believer plays in interpreting Christian existence.

As is well known, Bultmann was influenced in developing his position by William Wrede's view that Mark had no personal knowledge of Jesus' life, even though he might have had some idea of its historical basis. Jesus' history in Mark, says Wrede, is interwoven with beliefs of the primitive church. The idea that Jesus is the bearer of a certain dignity, a higher supernatural being who keeps the "Messianic secret" to himself, is based upon early church interpretations of the meaning of his life, death and resurrection. Therefore, the Gospel of Mark already belongs to the history of dogma. [9]

Peter is reported to have said in his sermon at Pentecost: "God has made him both Lord and Christ, this Jesus whom you crucified." (Acts 2:36) Wrede believes one must add to this affirmation the words *through the resurrection.* In his earthly life Jesus lacked the power and authority of the Messianic ruler. Paul seems to support this view: "By his resurrection from the dead" was Jesus "designated Son of God in power." (Rom. 1:4) The view that Jesus became the Messiah *only after his death* is, according to Wrede, the oldest of which we know. Had the earthly life of Jesus been regarded as Messianic, one would hardly have hit upon the idea later to regard the resurrection as the formal commencement of his Messiahship.

Wrede assumes that the Messianic material of the Gospels was non-existent for Paul. In Paul's eyes, apart from death and resurrection, Jesus' earthly life had little significance, except that it was like unto that of a slave (cf. Phil. 2:7ff.).[10] The idea of a secret Messiahship must have developed at a later time.

Wrede, attempting to grasp the inner rationale of the Gospels, particularly that of Mark, saw the early church theologizing in an oral tradition in which the historical accuracy of an individual report became relatively uncertain. He realized that the account of the Gospel of Mark was dogmatic, but instead of drawing out the specifically theological implications of this insight, he stressed the role of the believer in the process of interpretation. It was this factor that was to become the dominant element in Bultmann's form criticism. Would it not have been possible for Wrede, seeing the dogmatic issue involved in the Gospel of Mark, to inquire about the reality of God in the resurrection? What was the specifically theological problem that might have demanded a reinterpretation of Jesus' life in Messianic terms? Wrede set the course for a man-centered interpretation of the Gospels in which the specifically theological problem—what God has to do with Jesus—becomes a coordinate rather than a primary concern. It is not too difficult to see a parallel between James M. Robinson's stress on man's quest for meaningful existence and Wrede's stress on the human factor in the shaping of the Gospel.

Birger Gerhardsson has recently suggested that form criticism works with a completely wrong historical presupposition. Its reconstruction of the oral tradition of primitive Christianity is said to disregard the limits imposed upon it by the actual process of oral tradition in Judaism and Hellenism. Tradition was "for different groups both in Judaism and in the Hellenistic world . . . a concept, a deliberate concept, an important concept. The same is true in early Christianity." [11] There were long-established patterns which formed the oral and written traditions. The primitive church as a part of Judaism had little choice in the matter.

Gerhardsson contends that originally the apostles were not traveling and proclaiming the Gospel at all. They formed a kind of college in Jerusalem where they taught. In their *didache* in Jerusalem they were working on the tradition that originated in Jesus. It was handed down in the early church in a definite form. In this very form it furnished the basis of the *kerygma*. [12]

Thus for Gerhardsson the idea that the Christology of the New Testament is a creation of the early church seems historically improbable. Jesus, very much like Jewish and Hellenistic teachers of his day, "must have made his disciples learn certain sayings by heart; if he taught, he must have required his disciples to memorize." As faithful students the disciples would not have tried to change Jesus' teachings. [13]

This does not mean that interpretation did not occur in the primitive church. But it did not materially change Jesus' teaching. In his earthly ministry Jesus was only partly able to communicate to his disciples the meaning of his work. After the resurrection he taught them anew, so that they were "completely enabled to understand the witness of the Scriptures concerning him." [14]

Gerhardsson is attacking a particular historico-causal reconstruction of the oral tradition of primitive Christianity. While his own reconstruction of Christian origins may curtail the subjectivism of the view he opposes, systematic theology must realize that its task only begins at this point. Even if the view of the early church that Jesus was the Messiah had something to do with Jesus' self-understanding, as Gerhardsson claims, what does such historical knowledge amount to as regards our understanding of God? That Jesus might have had a Messianic self-consciousness is a mere matter of historical information and as such says nothing about God. Systematic theology has to listen to what historical study in the origins of Christianity has to say. But it has to consider the results on another level of argument.

Systematic theology must grasp the limitation of historical study at this point. The historical view of Jesus can teach systematic theology that Jesus was immersed in the historical process. It can instruct us why the assessment of the process is ambiguous. It can show us where this ambiguity is most oppressive. But history does not tell us why a particular historical event should point beyond itself to God. It is not at all a matter of course that Jesus should be understood as the revelation of the very heart of reality, or as God speaking, or as the illumination of the word "God." We thus need to grasp the hermeneutical rationale of the primitive church for viewing God and Jesus together. The merely "historical" approach to Jesus Christ does not give us an answer. A brief consideration of the radically factual view of Jesus will further substantiate this point.

JESUS AS HISTORICAL FACT

Hardly a theologian in the twentieth century has tried more vigorously to refute the view of Jesus as an interpretation than Albert Schweitzer, although he realized that there were remarkable similarities between his position and that of Wrede. He wrote that the coincidence between his *Sketch of the Life of Jesus* (the forerunner of *The Quest of the Historical Jesus*) and Wrede's book "is not more surprising in regard to the time of their appearance than in regard to the character of their contents. They appeared upon the self-same day, their titles are almost identical, and their agreement in the criticism of the modern historical conception of the life of Jesus extends sometimes to the very phraseology. And yet they are written from quite different standpoints, one from the point of view of literary criticism, the other from that of the historical recognition of eschatology." [15] Central for Schweitzer as for Wrede was the most accurate possible historico-critical assessment of Mark's Gospel.

Schweitzer differs from Wrede in his conviction that the lack of chronological and logical sequence in the Marcan account properly reflects historical fact: the erratic behavior of Jesus is determined by late Jewish apocalyptic thought; eschatological doctrines provide the pattern for Jesus' decisions. Opposing Wrede, Schweitzer asks "whether the dogmatic element is not precisely the historical element." Schweitzer understands eschatology, the framework in which Jesus acted, as dogmatic history, a history "moulded by theological beliefs—which breaks in upon the natural course of history and abrogates it." [16]

Whether Schweitzer says that Jesus was dominated by a "dogmatic idea" or "dogmatic considerations," he is pointing to the same rationale of Jesus' action. He discovers the dogmatic element throughout the Gospel narrative. While for Wrede the resolve to suffer and to die is also dogmatic, but therefore "unhistorical, and only to be explained by a literary hypothesis," for Schweitzer the resolve is "dogmatic, and therefore historical." [17] The dogmatic element is always to be explained by the eschatological doctrines current in Jesus' day.[18]

Schweitzer makes it emphatically clear that he experiences the eschatological Jesus as an offense. Jesus' eschatological views cannot be meaningful for modern man in a direct way. Jesus erred in his expectation of a near end. But we do not need the eschatological Jesus. We can understand him today in a few of his pithy sayings. He wanted to change the world. We can will the same thing. Here the question of Jesus' relationship to God is not raised at all. Schweitzer was satisfied to have ascertained the facts. As to Jesus' significance for him, he was content with a spiritual understanding of his person.

The lack of a specifically theological concern in Schweitzer's view of the historical Jesus became especially apparent when Martin Werner drew out the implications of Schweitzer's position for the history of dogma. He took form criticism to task for trying to interpret the Gospels as products of the oral tradition of the primitive church *without* raising the question what *the actual course of events* might have been. Inquiry into the original life situation, the "Sitz im Leben," of a particular passage calls for some historical criticism in any case. It ought to be applied more consistently. One should ask under what circumstances such a passage appeared. In order to answer the question one has to have a reliable *criterion of historicity* which is lacking in form criticism.

Werner found this criterion—following Schweitzer's view of

"consistent eschatology"—in the framework of late Jewish apocalyptic thought. Jesus shared the idea of a transformation of the
world in the near future. Primitive Christianity had the same
outlook toward the future as Jesus. But the outlook was transformed, since the cataclysmic events that had been expected did
not occur.[19]

In order to make some adjustment for the "mistake" in
eschatological doctrine, unhistorical elements were introduced
into the secondary reports of the resurrection appearances in the
Gospel accounts. In I Corinthians 15, the early Pauline report,
all that happens is that Jesus appears to the disciples as the risen
one. In the secondary resurrection accounts of the Gospels,
parousia or eschatological motifs have been injected: angels appear and the Messianic banquet is celebrated. The apostolic
age had turned out not to have been the final age. Therefore Jesus'
death and resurrection were more and more reinterpreted in terms
of the eschatological expectation. More and more Christian
doctrine deeschatologized the original expectation of the end until
in modern times the relevance of the expectation was completely
discarded in many quarters of the church.

Werner's criterion of historicity seems to center in Jesus'
mistake in assessing the eschatological doctrine, a mistake that
demanded continuous doctrinal amendment in the church. Christian doctrine, at least in its root, thus appears to have nothing to
do with God, but only with human error. Martin Werner reached
the end of the road in the development that asked the question
of the criterion of historicity without ever raising the question of
God.

Some of this Felix Flückiger sensed in his critique of the
Schweitzer-Werner position of a decade ago.[20] His major point
of criticism was based on a different reconstruction of the originating events of the Christian faith. He attacked the view that
Jesus in sacrificing himself wanted to introduce the delayed coming of the kingdom.

Delighted, however, with Schweitzer's thesis that the historical Jesus is the "dogmatic" Jesus, Flückiger claims that
Schweitzer proved the dogmatic view of the church to have been
proper. Messianic dogmatics—Christology—was actually the core

of Jesus' life and thought. Since Jesus' Messiahship lies at the center of the Gospel, there was good reason for the development of the christological formulas of the church. Jesus testified to himself as the Messiah who would bring the kingdom. On this presupposition the preaching of the church also became Messianic.

With this understanding Flückiger wishes to deepen Schweitzer's thesis. The dogmatic history of which Schweitzer speaks did not stop with the late Jewish expectations of the end. The Judge was expected to come. But the one who came was the Savior. The victory of grace over judgment is the innermost nucleus of the dogmatic history of Jesus. Schweitzer's and Werner's "consistent eschatology" eliminate the grace motif. How could the Gospel arise as the good news of salvation? Flückiger argues that Jesus understood himself as the Paschal Lamb sacrificed for the sins of the many. Dogma formation already began in Jesus' soteriological view of his death. The Gospels do not tell the "life of Jesus," but the Passion of the Messiah.

Jewish apocalyptic thought did not expect a period of grace before the day of wrath, but the Gospel does. The great turning point in early Christian history did not come in the post-apostolic age, but already in Jesus' Messianic work. God made Jesus take the final judgment upon himself as the rejected Messiah.[21] Jesus' life became realized eschatology. His Messianic work is the starting point and core of Christian dogma. It is not a future work, but the fulfilled work of salvation in incarnation, death and resurrection.[22]

In claiming that God made Jesus take the final judgment upon himself, Flückiger no longer speaks in strictly historico-causal terms. He introduces a new factor in his picture of Jesus by asking a question different from that of Schweitzer and Werner. Schweitzer, Flückiger charges, looks at Jesus from the viewpoint of the modern activist who believes in a goal of history. The coming of the kingdom is made dependent on human effort. But here one also has to reveal the presupposition of Schweitzer's view. He was not concerned about Jesus' relationship to God, but merely about Jesus as a human being. At this point the criticism of the modern historical view of Jesus has to be pressed beyond Schweitzer. Perhaps the inconsistencies in the Gospel accounts are not so much due to the erratic eschatological consciousness of Jesus as to man's difficulty in seeing God involved in Jesus' history.

Our two sections on Jesus as interpretation and Jesus as historical fact may seem to have resulted in little more than a cataloging of historical opinions. What keeps our overview from being an exercise in futility? Systematic theology must "zero in" on the point in Jesus' history where God and man were seen joined together by the primitive church. Only a continual reexamination of the innumerable data supplied by historical research in the origins of Christianity leads us to seek the *one* central datum. Systematic theology must pursue its task in continuity with Jesus research. It must feel the full impact of the search of historical studies to find a unifying center in the life of Jesus. Recent Protestant theology reflects serious wrestling with this issue. The new quest of God, however, demands that it be made more explicit.

A CENTRAL DATUM OF HERMENEUTICAL CONCERN?

The most important objections to the historico-causal reconstruction of the historical Jesus from the viewpoint of the new quest of the historical Jesus have been summarized by James M. Robinson in his book on the new quest.[23] During the development of a theology oriented in form criticism "it became increasingly clear that 'the historical Jesus,' the scholarly reconstruction of Jesus' biography by means of objective historical method, was . . . an attempt to build one's existence upon that which is under man's control and invariably at his disposal. The historical Jesus as a proven divine fact is a worldly security with which the *homo religiosus* arms himself in his effort to become self-sufficient before God, just as did the Jew in Paul's day by appeal to the law." [24] The alternative position which grew out of Wrede's literary criticism is content with Jesus as an interpretation and concentrates on the *kerygma*, the message about him: "The term *kerygma* comes to represent the unifying element in the contemporary situation: historically speaking, the central content of primitive Christian preaching was God's eschatological action centring in the saving event of cross and resurrection. Theologically speaking, this saving event proclaimed by the *kerygma* shows itself to be eschatological precisely by recurring in the proclamation of the *kergyma* itself: the act of proclaiming Jesus' death and resurrection becomes God's act calling upon me to accept my death and receive resurrected life." [25]

Robinson seeks to move beyond both approaches. His essay proposing a new quest of the historical Jesus has become one of the germinative events in contemporary New Testament studies and systematic theology as well. We presuppose knowledge of the detail of his argument and briefly lift out the basic concepts of his view.

Robinson does not want to study Jesus' life in a merely historico-causal way, but also does not intend to disregard what might be ascertained as historical of Jesus' words and deeds. He is convinced "that Jesus' understanding of his existence, his selfhood, and thus in the higher sense his life, is a possible subject of historical research." The twentieth century has a new understanding of history: "A new quest must be built upon the fact that the sources *do* make possible a new kind of quest working in terms of the modern view of history and the self." [26] The *kerygma* is not discarded as insignificant, but its truth is controlled by an encounter with Jesus mediated by the new approach to history: "A quest of the historical Jesus involves an attempt to disengage information about the historical Jesus from its kerygmatic colouring, and thus to mediate an encounter with the historical Jesus distinct from the encounter with the *kerygma*." [27] Thus we are supposedly offered some certainty that the *kerygma* is not dealing with a myth.

If one follows James M. Robinson's argument closely, one finds that his concern for the historical Jesus centers in one basic historical datum, the flesh of the incarnation. The stress on the incarnation makes us face an offense: "In the encounter with Jesus one is confronted with the *skandalon*." The *skandalon* is the fact that we meet in Jesus' "all-too-human Jewish eschatological message the eternal word of God." [28] Here a factor is introduced that greatly sharpens the quest of the historical Jesus. God's involvement in history is now viewed as a component of the central historical datum. The unusual aspect of this development is that it is introduced from the perspective of the historian. It is, as it were, a finding of historical research. Here we meet a major problem.

From our review of the research in Christian origins and the life of Jesus we can learn that each approach converges upon a center around which it organizes its basic understanding of the issue involved, located either in the *kerygma* or in the historical Jesus himself. For Wrede it is the resurrection; for Bultmann, cross and resurrection. Schweitzer and Werner appeal to Jesus' Messianic self-consciousness. Flückiger's basic historical datum is quite similar, although he also stresses the cross. Gerhardsson, to the extent that we are able to discover his views in this respect, again points to Jesus' self-consciousness. James M. Robinson, also converging in his thought on an organizing center, moves beyond the historical framework of these data into *a new dimension*. The sharpening of the historical quest ought to be clear. What is at stake now is not merely the authenticity of this or that facet of Jesus' thought and work, but also the possibility of an encounter with God through him. Hugh Anderson observes this as a trend in the new quest of the historical Jesus as a whole: "Thus Bornkamm speaks of men's confrontation with the immediacy of God's presence in the words (and deeds) of Jesus . . . Fuchs and Ebeling [speak] of experiencing in Jesus the ground of the Word of God." [29] The new quest of God demands that this trend become the central theme at least of systematic theology.

In a review article on the debate triggered by *Honest to God*, Martin E. Marty quotes Bishop Robinson: "The affirmation of the New Testament that he who has seen Jesus has seen the Father is *not* a statement that the whole quest for the Father is futile, but that men have no need to look *further* for the Father. For in Jesus they *have* a revelation of ultimate Reality: 'No one has ever seen God; but God's only Son, he who is nearest to the Father's heart, he has made him known.' " [30] Then Marty goes on to state a critical point: "Robinson, in citing Scripture and making these declarations has, as it were, described the rules of the game, but he has not yet played it. The time for beginnings is here." [31] What is the game? It is finding *God* in Jesus. Here *the new quest of the historical Jesus and the new quest of God meet*. All the historical quest finally amounts to is a confrontation with Jesus as a historical factor with little more significance than other historical factors unless his witness to God is taken into consideration.

At the point where the new quest of the historical Jesus and the new quest of God meet, the hermeneutical question becomes especially pressing. The present situation in Protestant theology demands that the relationship between history and God be thought through once more, now with the full realization that the understanding of God is the aim of the hermeneutical query. This cannot be done, however, without an explicit articulation of the dialectic between history and God.

In James M. Robinson the dialectic does not become very apparent, since he does not go much beyond the evaluating of historical data once he has pointed to the need for man's encounter with God in Jesus. It is more tangible in an essay by Gerhard Ebeling on "The Question of the Historical Jesus and the Problem of Christology." [32] For Ebeling as well, the appreciation of the historical Jesus is not a matter of mere historical fact. He believes a concept of history must be employed that is adequate to the objective of the investigation. The concept itself is shaped by the question that guides the historical inquiry: "That does not mean that the concept of fact could be done without altogether. But we must be clear as to the limits within which it is justified. The only thing that can lead us out of the historical difficulty is the view of history which takes its bearings on the word-event and consequently on the linguisticality of reality. Hence the proper question regarding the past is not: What happened? What were the facts? How are they to be explained? or something of that kind, but: What came to expression?"

What came to expression in the life of Jesus, according to Ebeling, was faith. It is the one datum upon which all the other aspects of Jesus' life converge. The centrality of faith in Jesus' life rules out concern for chronological and psychological detail: "And it can rank indeed as a result of this concentration of Jesus upon the coming to expression of faith that he himself has rendered superfluous all interest in exact biographical detail or psychological presentation." But while the concentration on faith rules out interest in historical detail, it implies the concern for

God as the referent of faith: "Faith as such is directed towards God as the act of entering into relations with . . . God. To believe in Jesus therefore means: to enter into relations with God in view of him, . . . to participate in him and his ways and consequently to participate in what faith is promised participation in, namely, the omnipotence of God." Unless we misread Ebeling's essay, its entire point would seem to be to call attention to the understanding of God that is mediated through Jesus' faith. Therefore the question Ebeling is asking of Jesus' history is actually a very specific question: Did *God* come to expression? The understanding that faith as such is directed toward God is not simply the *result* of Ebeling's investigation. God is already presupposed in the question. Ebeling wants to know what faith in God means on the basis of Jesus' relationship to him.

Ebeling's concept of history already implies God as a factor. Here things become extremely complex. Ebeling wishes to reflect the posture of modern man: "[If] modern man's understanding of reality takes its bearings so decidedly on the historical and worldly nature of the world, then we should be doing that understanding of reality a decided service by learning to speak in truly historical and truly worldly ways of God." [33] The world itself has to be understood as history. Ebeling apparently tries to keep God and world, God and history, separate, finding their unity only in the word-event. They unite only *as they witness to the cross.*[34] But why should one's concern for God finally center on the cross? Does history as such suggest the cross as a hermeneutically central datum? Perhaps faith in the cross depends as little on a modern concept of history as on a factual reconstruction of the life of Jesus.

HISTORY AS ABSOLUTE

What results when the modern concept of history becomes the sole orientation point of faith can be seen in Carl Michalson's *The Rationality of Faith,* a 1963 publication. The purpose of the book is to demonstrate the significance of the modern concept of history for the Christian faith. Michalson tries to show "how it comes about that Christians and non-Christians alike impute to Christianity absurdities which are not really there, and how these absurdities may evaporate and give way to solidly redemptive meaning when the question of Christian understanding is rigorously set within the logic of history." The rationality of faith consists in the absence of absurdities, if faith is approached on the model of history. Michalson hopes to adopt history as "the model for theological thinking." [35]

The distinctive mark of Michalson's view is the incommensurability of history with nature. There is no reason to object to the analogy between history and faith. But must history be the ultimate court of appeal? Michalson also uses the word "God," equating it, however, with history or one of its facets. There is no God to appeal to beyond history: "There is no immediate relation between Christians and God: that relation is mediated by Jesus of Nazareth, the word of God." Every aspect of God's being or activity relates to history: "The everlasting arms are made of history, the fleshiness of the lived world." [36] Knowledge of God is not obtainable from nature but only from historical events: the resurrection, for example, he views as an event "in which it is revealed through Jesus of Nazareth who God really is." [37] Truly to know God means to have a new relationship to the world: "The word 'God' is not an invitation to point to some transcendent reality. It is an invocation to receive the world from beyond oneself." [38]

For Michalson history is interpretation. So is theology: "The task of the theologian, like that of the historian, is to stir up the sentiment of meaning in the sedimentation of events." [39] The task of theology consists in working out the proper relationship between fact and meaning.

If history is the ultimate court of appeal, one wonders why reference to God should be made at all. While history might make faith seem more rational and less absurd and thus might function as an *analogy* of theological thought, by itself it is unable to give meaning to the word "God." In Michalson history, in fact, has become a substitute for God. He acknowledges, at least by implication, the "death of God."

As regards the stress on the historical dimension of the Christian faith, the position of van Buren is very similar to that of Michalson. Van Buren selects a number of features of the new quest of the historical Jesus in order to undergird his historical view of the Christian faith. Concentrating especially on Jesus' freedom, van Buren employs a historical view of this freedom as a substitute for the concept of God: "The word 'God' has been avoided because it equivocates and misleads. It seems to be a proper name, calling up the image of a divine entity, but it refuses to function as any other proper name does." [40]

Van Buren suggests that Jesus' freedom can become the pattern of life for the contemporary believer. But what is the point of Jesus' freedom in the New Testament? Even if one only superficially looks at the Fourth Gospel, the Gospel so dear to van Buren, one must notice that its primary concern is to show Jesus' freedom *for* God. Van Buren regards Jesus as "the model of full manhood." [41] But is not Jesus as the model of full manhood a secondary concern in the Fourth Gospel and subject to his being the image of *God?* The Fourth Gospel shows Jesus interpreting God as God: "No man has ever seen God; but God's only Son, he who is nearest to the Father's heart, he has made him known." (John 1:18. NEB) Whom has Jesus made known? Himself? Jesus does not speak about himself for his own sake— to show what freedom is or who man is—but to confront man with God and in this encounter to let man find his true self. He first of all points away from himself.

Jesus' freedom, in van Buren's view, is supposed to invite men to become authentically free. Free for whom? The point of the Fourth Gospel and, for that matter, of the entire New Testament is that man cannot make the move from bondage to freedom unless he is freed from himself for God. When history is made absolute, man is ultimately left alone.

THE HISTORICAL APORIA

As man tries to come to grips with his primal experience of being, he seeks to find a word for it. We noted the aporia that results. The appeal to the historical dimension relative to Jesus

Christ also leads to an aporia. It would be pointless to make the historico-critical method responsible for it. Historico-critical research confronts us with the bare historicity of Jesus of Nazareth. There is nothing puzzling about Jesus' historicity as such. The problem begins when history and God are viewed together.[42] Why should man be confronted with God in the history of one man? As we have seen, the particularity of the question is even more specific: Why should man be confronted *with God in a man on a cross?*

James M. Robinson speaks of the theological permissiveness of the new quest of the historical Jesus.[43] The present interest in the Jesus of history found its first precedent in the writing of the Gospels: since the primitive church turned from the risen Christ back to the Jesus of history, we, too, are permitted to turn to Jesus. Of course, the theological meaning of this reverting to Jesus must be explicated: the Christ of faith does not reflect a myth, but the meaning of a historical person. Robinson as exegete and historian soon moves from the examination of the theological permissiveness of the new quest to other concerns. But the systematic theologian has to pause here and ponder the implications of *the historiography of the primitive church* for the church today. James M. Robinson believes that primitive Christianity "experienced Jesus as a unique action of God." Systematic theology must discover the present-day implications of this historical experience. It must grasp the hermeneutical process involved in New Testament historiography and translate it into a contemporary hermeneutic.[44] If the New Testament converges on the cross as the central datum of hermeneutical concern, it may well be that it does this not because it begins with interest in historical fact or in history in general, but because it raises the question of God in a unique way.

The cross, however, does not furnish a direct answer to man's ontological aporia. Tillich speaks of Christ becoming "completely transparent to the mystery he reveals." [45] But there is a note in the New Testament that Tillich does not mention as a significant factor. Before Jesus goes to the cross, he says to his disciples: "All ye shall be offended because of me this night." (Matt. 26:31. King James) There is nothing divine in the offense as such. The point is that Jesus on the cross is not transparent to the mystery he reveals. If God was involved in the cross, it certainly was *incognito*.

Can the cross be an event which is the final touchstone of faith and action, a *primordial deed*? A deed on which all Christian faith and action depend, a deed that conquers death and generates life? Does the life preceding the cross lift God's *incognito*? Are there factors in the life that interpret the cross? Can God also be grasped in the ministry of Jesus? Does Jesus' life belong to the primordial deed as much as his death?

The primitive church apparently experienced an aporia in the face of Jesus' cross. Ernst Fuchs writes of the aporia: "The cross made one realize that one was thrown upon God." [46] All historical research can do at this point is to articulate the aporia. [47]

In his recently published outlines of Christology, Wolfhart Pannenberg has taken a different tack. The work as a whole is a magisterial reconstruction of Christology which does not have its like in recent Protestant theology. It is especially remarkable for its lucidity. We only wish to focus briefly on its major methodological premise. For Pannenberg God's revelation in Jesus can be asserted only in view of his resurrection from the dead. He distinguishes his position from two others: (1) Jesus' unity with God is already revealed in the sovereign claim of his proclamation and action; and (2) The resurrection reveals only what Jesus already accomplished on the cross. [48]

According to Pannenberg the resurrection contains an incontrovertible evidence whose meaning we cannot doubt. We can know the meaning of the resurrection in the context of our knowledge of the apocalyptic expectation. By contrast the cross lacks perspicuity in every respect. Jesus' death taxed the faith of the disciples to the utmost. The cross was a defeat. It belonged to those events that are utterly puzzling. [49] There is no evidence in the New Testament, however, that the resurrection was felt to have been less puzzling. The meaning of the resurrection is not something that everyone can read off the bare events of history, if only he uses the right method. [50]

History as such does not directly speak of God, in a resurrection as little as in a cross. We have little choice but to join the disciples in their movement from one historical aporia (the cross) to the other historical aporia (the resurrection). Perhaps the story of the disciples on the road to Emmaus can serve as a model. The women had told the story of the resurrection to the apostles. But "these words seemed to them an idle tale, and they did not believe them." (Luke 24:11) Afterwards when Jesus appeared to two of the disciples on the road to Emmaus, "their eyes were kept from recognizing him." (Luke 24:16) Only after the resurrected one himself had interpreted the Scriptures ("Was it not necessary that Christ should suffer these things and enter into glory?"—Luke 24:26) and had given them a sign in the breaking of the bread were their eyes opened. Thus in the resurrection the meaning of the suffering was interpreted. Without a grasp of the unity of cross and resurrection interpreted by the reality to which they point the resurrection remains mute.

Historical interpretation and historical fact are fused in the biblical texts. Where history itself shows that the theological question is unanswerable in terms of either historical interpretation or historical fact, systematic theology begins. As a historical datum the resurrection underlines the puzzlement of God's involvement in history. On purely historical grounds it is quite unintelligible why a resurrection should tell us more about God than a cross. On the plane of history we are forced to view the end of Jesus' life in terms of the radical historical limitations of every man's life: "The end *might* be a death without significance—as well as being the end of the road of possibility." [51]

Of course, Pannenberg is right when he tries to view God and resurrection together. But the interpretation that makes God meaningful in the resurrection transcends the merely historical interpretation.[52] The "inner history" of the resurrection is as little available to man on purely historical grounds as the "inner history" of Jesus' life or of his death. The merely historical view of Jesus is fraught with a definite limitation.[53]

Anyone who has been able to view the film *The Parable* (commissioned by the Protestant Council of the City of New York for the 1964 World's Fair) has had an opportunity to puzzle about the historical aporia. Mostly a pantomime for its twenty-two minutes, the film presents a clown who "all white-on-white from flowing robes to chalky Marcel Marceau makeup" [54] goes through a number of motions that intend to reflect actions of Christ, or so it seems. The obviously "silly" acts and the pointless death of the clown as well as his presence after death hardly convey an immediately intelligible point. Almost brutally the film confronts the viewer with the major aspect of the dilemma Christ's contemporaries must have faced: Is there an "other dimension" in Christ's history that is not directly noticeable? He is said to have laid claim to an "other dimension." To view *The Pawnbroker* and *The Parable* in sequence, as it were, is to be confronted with the primal hermeneutical quandary of theology: Does *The Parable* have anything to say to *The Pawnbroker*, the historical aporia to the ontological aporia, Christ to man, that is not directly tangible on the plane of history? [55]

HISTORICO-ONTOLOGICAL HERMENEUTIC IN THE FOURTH GOSPEL

Christ . . . was the greatest artist of all, disdaining marble, clay or colour, working with living flesh. That is to say that this unbelievable artist, one who is scarcely conceivable to such an obtuse instrument as the modern neurotic, worn-out brain, made neither statues, nor pictures, nor books; indeed, he said clearly enough what he was doing— fashioning living men, immortal beings. . . .

Christ, this great artist, though he disdained books written about ideas . . . never . . . disdained the spoken word. . . .

These spoken words, which, like a great prodigal lord, he did not even deign to write down, are one of the highest peaks, the highest in fact ever reached by art, which there becomes a creative force, a pure creative force.

Such considerations as these . . . take us a long way, a very long way: they raise us even above art. They enable one to catch a glimpse of the art of creating life, the art of living immortality.[1]

VINCENT VAN GOGH

OUR inquiry thus far has resulted in nothing more than the articulation of the ontological and the historical aporiae. The first aporia reflects man's inability to come to grips with his experience of being. The second grows out of the problem of New Testament historiography. It is now necessary to show in what way these aporiae that appeared from the very beginning of the Christian faith might be related.

The Fourth Gospel today is often used to undergird contemporary theological positions. Martin E. Marty tracked down the rules of the game for *The Honest to God Debate* in Bishop Robinson's appeal to John 1:18: "No one has ever seen God; but God's only Son, he who is nearest to the Father's heart, he has made him known." Bishop Robinson believes that the Fourth Gospel in making this affirmation does not wish to suggest that the whole quest for the Father is futile, but rather that there is no other place to meet the Father except in Jesus of Nazareth. In his latest book, *The New Reformation?*, in which he discusses the possibility that we might be living in the age of a new Reformation, Bishop Robinson again appeals to the Fourth Gospel and even goes so far as to say: "Indeed, if any text proves central to the new Reformation, as Luther's *sola fide* was to the old, I predict that it will be John 14:9: 'He who has seen me has seen the Father.' For this is its point of entry. To talk about 'God' may, to many, be meaningless; to ask, with Philip, 'Show us the Father,' may appear a futile metaphysical question. But all the old questions of *theology* can find their focus and come to rest in this *man*." [2] Paul van Buren uses the Fourth Gospel to support a more radical thesis: the quest for the Father is pointless.[3] Although James M. Robinson does not use the Fourth Gospel to support the new quest of the historical Jesus, he feels that it is this Gospel which has most radically grasped the problem of the historiography of the primitive church.

Testimonies to the significance of the Fourth Gospel in the present debate could be multiplied.[4] All we wish to ascertain in the following pages is its significance for finding *a hermeneutical rationale of New Testament historiography*. It would be of interest also to examine the other Gospels in this respect. But only the Fourth Gospel prefaces its story with a hermeneutical introduction. The prologue, John 1:1–18, is a brief hermeneutic. Can the hermeneutic of the Fourth Gospel teach us anything for the present hermeneutical debate? The model of Christian theology might be found neither in history nor in linguistic analysis or a general ontology, but in its own origins.

HISTORY IN THE FOURTH GOSPEL

Central to Edwyn C. Hoskyns' commentary on the Fourth Gospel is the tenet that God is the basic referent of its historiography. In view of the recent concourse of the new quest of the historical Jesus with the new quest of God this becomes of primary import, insofar as the design of the Fourth Gospel is to relate the most important facets of Jesus' history, his signs and his words, to God.

Hoskyns believes that even the most cursory reading of the Fourth Gospel will make one realize that it differs from the Synoptics in significant ways. It contains a much more limited selection of events from Jesus' life. There is no real equivalent to the Synoptic parables. Jesus' message of the Kingdom of God finds no significant place. Eschatology has lost its original setting. This does not mean, however, "that in the Fourth Gospel all touch with history has been surrendered, and surrendered purposely." [5] Hoskyns is able to adduce considerable support for his thesis that the writer of the Fourth Gospel "falls back on words, phrases and even whole sentences that are characteristic of the earlier tradition, and in particular of the tradition in its Marcan form." But it is also obvious that "the author of the Fourth Gospel is not content to leave this knowledge in the form in which it was already possessed by his readers." [6] He did not report in terms of what an eyewitness apprehended of the Jesus of history, but of what the believers saw in Jesus. The author tries to interpret Jesus of Nazareth in the context of the witness of the church. Hoskyns wants us to keep in mind John 20:30f.: "Now Jesus did many other signs in the presence of the disciples, which are not written in this book; but these are written that you may believe that Jesus is the Christ, the Son of God, and that believing you may have life in his name." The Fourth Gospel was written, whether by an eyewitness or not, for the purpose of interpreting to the readers Jesus *as the Christ, the Son of God.* At least this is what it articulates as its purpose. It does not intend to be a chronicle of events.

The qualifier "Son of God" points to the core problem of primitive Christian historiography. The relationship of the manhood of Jesus to his divine Sonship became the touchstone of theological thought. It is not an innovation of the fourth evangelist. In Hoskyns' view it is "a basic theme of the Pauline Epistles (cf. Gal. 4:3–7) and of the Epistle to the Hebrews (2:5–18) and, in the end, of the synoptic tradition also, when the analysis of the subject-matter is pressed beyond a technical examination of the characteristic terminology with which the Evangelists are operating." [7] What captivated primitive Christian thought was the question of how a man could have that close a relationship to God. It did not find the answer on the merely historical plane: "This is what the Fourth Evangelist makes so clear in order that all possible misunderstanding may be avoided. Jesus is the Son of God, not because He as a man claimed to be so, but because God sent Him into the world as His Son." [8] God's sending of Jesus of Nazareth involves a dimension which is not commensurate with objective history.

Hoskyns is of the opinion that beginning with John 1:34 the witness to the Sonship is the basic theme of the Fourth Gospel. The Messiahship is defined in terms of divine Sonship. But in order to speak of the divine Sonship of this particular man, Christian thought had to come to grips with a grave problem. Jesus' life ended in "apparent failure." What sense does it make to say that God was involved in this failure? If the failure should be part of God's involvement in this man, it demands a unique way of describing it. Thus the fourth evangelist leaves out the agony of Gethsemane and the transfiguration as *specific incidents*, and, instead, "the heavenly glory of Jesus and His troubled humiliation are shown to condition every part of His life." It would be pointless, however, to note the fusion of the Gethsemane agony with the Gospel as a whole without revealing the specific reason: "The travail of Gethsemane is removed back into the body of the gospel. From the beginning the utter dependence of the Son upon the Father is rigorously maintained (e.g. 4:34, 5:30, 6:38). The Son does not seek His own glory (8:50). This antithesis is consciously held together everywhere. . . . The episodes of Transfiguration and Agony . . . woven together in one consistent

whole . . . control the Christology of the Fourth Gospel." [9]
Hoskyns believes that the Fourth Gospel makes explicit what the
Synoptics already wished to stress by introducing the story of the
transfiguration as a reflection of "a relation between Jesus and the
Father, visible to no human eye, a relation which conditioned
His whole visible activity and which was partially apprehended,
but altogether misunderstood, by the disciples." [10]

Thus the problem of *finding God in Jesus* has been sharply
focused. It involves *articulating simultaneously what is visible and
what is invisible in Jesus of Nazareth.* In terms of method this
demands a re-description of Jesus' life "in a technically *non-historical* form." Hoskyns suggests that the historico-critical method generally is not sensitive to the problem of theology "which is to set
forth the non-historical truth that underlies all history and which
is almost apparent in the life and death of Jesus." [11] This means
that the central issue of primitive Christian thought, at least in
the Fourth Gospel, was *theological.* Christian thought in its very
beginnings *was forced to ask a question that was not historico-
causal.* Hoskyns can thus say that for theology there is a "difference between describing history simply in relation to history—
which is the procedure of the technical historian—and describing
history in its theological significance." [12] The methodological principle as expressed by Hoskyns seems to be widely acknowledged
as a possibility in contemporary Protestant theology. But is it
actually applied to present-day theological issues? Does one see
its significance for the hermeneutic of God?

We noted before that the so-called new quest of the historical Jesus is aware of the problem of the theological significance of
Jesus' life. As an effort in the field of exegetical theology, it is
bound to move more in the dimension of historico-causal research.
But to the extent that it appeals to the modern concept of history
as lodestar of its interpretation, it perhaps deflects the radically
theological question too soon. In any case, systematic theology
dare not shun its responsibility at that point. It must look at Christian origins *primarily under the guidance of the question of God.*
We can lift out the issues by appealing once more to the position
of James M. Robinson.

As regards the legitimacy of a new quest of the historical

Jesus, Robinson points also to New Testament historiography: "Although the methods of New Testament 'historiography' and modern historiography are quite different, the same or similar kerygmatic motives which produced the one could lead us to a legitimate use of the other. Thus the discussion of the theological meaning of writing Gospels explicates the theological *permissiveness* of a new quest." In this context Robinson also sees the special concern of the Fourth Gospel for the radical historicity of revelation: "In order to dramatize earthly, corporeal existence as the realm of revelation . . . the Fourth Gospel portrays present religious experience in terms of Jesus' life. The evangelist implements this purpose by drawing attention to the ambiguity, the offense, the hiddenness, which characterized the revelation even in Jesus' life, as if to say: Today it is the same." [13] While it is true that later religious experience certainly was in need of being related to the originating event of Christianity and, in fact, became important in the historiography of the Fourth Gospel, the hermeneutical problem of the Gospel is not made fully explicit in Robinson's discussion. What was the nature of the revelation of which Robinson speaks? How are we to understand that God was involved in the ambiguity of Jesus' life? The author of the Fourth Gospel has a specifically theological question in mind with which he approaches his material, and which is not necessarily identical with the needs of later religious experience. Regardless of what exegetical theology does at this point, systematic theology must articulate the specifically theological question and under its guidance examine the material.

As regards the formulation of the theological question, the Fourth Gospel has much to teach us. The intention of the fourth evangelist, in Hoskyns' words, "is to force his readers back upon the life of Jesus in the flesh and upon His death in the flesh, as *the place of understanding*." [14] Perhaps we are interpreting Hoskyns in the way he would wish when we say that the author of the Fourth Gospel forces his readers back upon the life of Jesus in the flesh *in the light of his death in the flesh*. And what is the understanding that Jesus' death in the flesh can convey? God, says Hoskyns, is "making sense of history." In fact, "the theme of the Fourth Gospel is the non-historical that makes sense of history, the infinite that makes sense of time, God who makes sense of men. . . . " [15] The problem of systematic theology begins where history and God meet, and the theologian has to describe God's involvement in the particularity of the man Jesus. Why was Jesus' history from the very beginning directed toward the cross, and why was this God's own history?

Although we have described how history "works" in the Fourth Gospel in Hoskyns' terms, we have not as yet focused the basic theological question as regards Jesus' history in its sharpest form: *Why was it that God and history were linked in the Gospel in the first place?* Why should one human being stir up so much concern? Why should this one human being make sense of history, or time, or man? Why should we turn to it as a primordial event, as the place of understanding all other historical events?

We noted before that the prologue of the Fourth Gospel (1:1–18) tries to give an interpretation of the theological rationale that underlies its historiography.[16] The fourth evangelist himself had questions when he pondered the historicity of Jesus, questions he could not answer as long as he projected them only on the screen of history.[17] As he engaged in trying to understand this particular history, he articulated his method. The history of Jesus, says Hoskyns, was the starting point for his reflection: "The prologue to the Fourth Gospel does not move *to* Jesus but *from* Him." There is a process of thought that leads up to the prologue: "The Evangelist . . . is confronted by the words of Jesus. But the words of Jesus are not isolated maxims, detached aphorisms, or disjointed commands, powerful, but without connected meaning. Because of their essential unity the Evangelist is pressed from the plural to the singular, from 'words' to word, and from a series of words to The Word." [18]

This could not have happened, however, unless the evangelist had remembered the quest for a primordial word, the Word, the *Logos*.[19] Viewed in relation to this awareness of a primordial quest, the particularity of Jesus' history took on the shape of a primordial deed. What man only vaguely sensed in his quest for meaning found a concrete answer in the shape of Jesus' deed: "And so history, a particular history, moves into the center of the picture; not, however, in such a manner that history now exists as a thing in itself. A particular history moves into the center of the picture in its transparent relation to the Word. . . ." The prologue thus defines the hermeneutic of the Fourth Gospel.[20] As soon as one sees that the basic features of this hermeneutic are *the relationship of a particular history to the Word*, one only has to take one more step of thought to see that the corroboration of history by the Word is related to the ontological aporia. The fourth evangelist in writing his Gospel merged his encounter with Jesus on the historical plane with his effort as a man of his time and place to understand reality as a whole.

THE ONTOLOGICAL DIMENSION OF THE FOURTH GOSPEL

Obviously the word "ontology" is not biblical. This does not mean, however, that the dimension to which it points is un-biblical. Paul Tillich has given a classical definition of ontology which includes biblical thought: "Ontology is not a speculative-fantastic attempt to establish a world behind the world; it is an analysis of those structures of being which we encounter in every meeting with reality. . . . The Bible itself always uses categories and concepts which describe the structure of experience." [21] In order to see that the Fourth Gospel, as a biblical book, also uses concepts that reflect man's encounter with being, one only has to examine their background. The ontological reflection is perhaps most manifest where Hellenistic influence can be detected. But the ontological element is also present in Hebrew thought; only it found different expression there.

The prologue of the Fourth Gospel immediately introduces the ontological issue. Speaking as a systematic theologian, Paul Tillich outlines its ontological dimension in a few sentences: "Only against the background of the universal Logos is the incarnate Logos a meaningful concept. Biblical religion has shown the ontological implications of one of its fundamental assertions in the prologue of the Fourth Gospel. Ontology is able to receive the christological question—the question of the place in which the universal Logos manifests itself. . . . To say that Jesus as the

Christ is the concrete place where the Logos becomes visible is an assertion of faith and can be made only by him who is grasped by the Christ as the manifestation of his ultimate concern. But it is not an assertion which contradicts or is strange to the search for ultimate reality." [22] Tillich in this context perhaps does not stress enough that the universal Logos of the time of the Fourth Gospel was not understood in the same way the universal Logos is viewed today. One has to be careful lest one make too quick a transition from the ancient concept of the Logos to the contemporary problem of the word. But a comparison between the present-day hermeneutic of the word and the hermeneutic of the Logos is inevitable at this point.

Tillich goes on to say: "Without knowing something about the nature of the word, without an ontology of the Logos, theology cannot interpret the speaking of God, the divine Word. But, if theology uses this insight into the ontological nature of the word, it can teach meaningfully about the nature of the divine Word, the Logos who is with God." [23] We noted before how man's primal experience leads him to search for a word that could articulate it. But contemporary man cannot associate the word as directly with God as Hellenistic or Hebrew thought. Contemporary man has to make explicit to himself the step that is implied in the juxtaposition of Logos and God in the Fourth Gospel. In our present situation we must first articulate the relationship between *word* and *being* before we can hope to make sense of the relationship between word and the word "God" or the idea of God.

Careful historical examination of the key concepts of the prologue might produce the link between the modern concerns and the ancient ontological quest. The most recent comprehensive study of the background of the thought patterns in the Fourth Gospel is that of C. H. Dodd. Examining hermetic literature, Philo, Rabbinic Judaism, Gnosticism and Mandaism, he tries to ascertain the most likely background of the Gospel's leading ideas. He believes the readers of the Gospel were prepared for understanding the prologue because of "previous acquaintance with the terms used." One must read the prologue with the Old Testament and Hellenistic backgrounds in mind: "While . . . the statements of the Prologue *might* be understood all through on the assumption that λόγος is the Word of the Lord in the Old Testament sense, yet it seems certain that any reader influenced by the thought of Hellenistic Judaism, directly or at a remove, would inevitably find suggested here a conception of the creative and revealing λόγος in many respects similar to that of Philo; and it is difficult not to think that the author intended this. His λόγος is not simply the uttered word or command of God; it is the meaning, plan or purpose of the universe, conceived as transcendent as well as immanent, as the thought of God, formed within the eternal Mind and projected into objectivity." [24]

We may therefore say that right at the beginning of the Gospel the author, by introducing the Logos concept, hopes to show how the God-idea is related to man's quest for meaning. Without the experience of being, one cannot understand the quest for meaning. It is on this score that present-day hermeneutic overlaps with the biblical hermeneutic.

The crucial hermeneutical bridge-building in the Fourth Gospel takes place before Jesus' story is told—certainly not as a subtle philosophical argument, but nonetheless in explicit theological articulation. This is not to say that the author himself developed his hermeneutic *before* he delved into the history of Jesus. The history, as the author sees it, is the basis of his hermeneutical insight. In terms of its chronological development in the author's mind, the prologue perhaps ought to appear as a postscript. But what might be *chronologically second* in this instance is *ontologically first*. Having pondered the ontological foundation of his Gospel, the author tries to show that the most intimate relationship exists between Jesus' history and the Word. Jesus claims man's quest for the primordial word. He is its true content. He overcomes man's ontological aporia. He illumines the God-idea. What man has tried to name in the experience of being as "God" now appears in a new light. Jesus is the interpreter of the God-idea, of every naming of man's primal experience. Thus he is called "Son of God."

Having faced the cross, the acme of meaninglessness from the viewpoint of historico-causal objectivity, the one who seeks truth turns back upon the life of Jesus and tries to understand it in terms of the categories of the ontological quest. This is no longer a strictly historico-causal examination of the life of Jesus, but *a dialogue between man's primordial quest for the word and the memory of Jesus' words and deeds.* Words man has used in trying to understand his quest of the primordial word are now related to Jesus' life. Besides Logos, "truth," for example, is such a word.

In the Fourth Gospel Jesus is viewed in the light of a specific understanding of truth. According to Dodd, the concept "truth" in the Fourth Gospel "rests upon common Hellenistic usage in which it hovers between the meanings of 'reality', or 'the ultimately real', and 'knowledge of the real'. On one side at least, the knowledge of God which is life eternal is an apprehension of ultimate reality." [25] Hellenistic thinking reflects on the ultimately real as it introduces the issue of truth. It is significant that the prologue shares in this reflection. For we can detect in it the specific pre-awareness which was brought to bear on the Christ event, even though the pre-awareness in the light of this event turns out to have been a lack of genuine understanding of truth. It is certainly not possible for us to get back into the Hellenistic experience of life in order to understand the Christ event. But we must ask whether understanding the Christ event today does not presuppose a similar pre-awareness of truth.

The Fourth Gospel found truth in the structure of Jesus' life. It found it, however, in such a fashion that his history was not merely interpreted by itself, but by the categories that man had developed in the quest of the ultimately real. Thus the basic hermeneutical endeavor of the Fourth Gospel is the merging of the historical and the ontological dimensions. It is a systematic methodology by which Jesus' life is interpreted, focusing on the relationship between God and man in the particularity of this man. If the hermeneutical principle is overlooked, the dialectical tension between the two poles, the historical and the ontological, is lost, and Jesus in the Fourth Gospel is regarded either as completely divine or completely human.[26] The point of the Fourth Gospel is to speak of the unity between God and man in the man Jesus. In order to make its point, it created its historico-ontological hermeneutic.

NONECCLESIASTICAL INTERPRETATION

Although the basic hermeneutical rationale of the Fourth Gospel can be adequately understood in terms of the historico-ontological dialectic, we cannot overlook the fact that the Fourth Gospel most likely was not engaged in a dialogue with pure Hellenism, but with Hellenistic Judaism. Along with its reinterpretation of ontological terminology we find a reinterpretation of the ecclesiastical terminology of Judaism. In fact, both are intimately interwoven most of the time. The signs of the Fourth Gospel were selected by its author to show "that Jesus is the Christ, the Son of God." (John 20:31) The Fourth Gospel applies the terms "Christ" and "Son of God" in a fashion not sanctified by the official theology of Judaism. This can be described as a nonecclesiastical interpretation, an effort purposely rejecting the accepted view of the ecclesiastical establishment of Judaism.

An essay by W. C. van Unnik on "The Purpose of St. John's Gospel" brings out this other aspect of the hermeneutical rationale of the Fourth Gospel quite clearly. Van Unnik objects to the current view of the purpose of the Fourth Gospel that fails to consider the principle the author himself declared to have been his lodestar in John 20:30f. Van Unnik claims that in Bultmann's *Theology of the New Testament* "one finds the discussion of the terms 'Christ' and 'Son of God' somewhere in a corner, but they do not function as the steering ideas." [27] What we have called a nonecclesiastical interpretation becomes a concern only if one takes note of the purpose of the Fourth Gospel expressed in John 20:30f.

Van Unnik points out that the Fourth Gospel is the only writing of the New Testament that uses the Hebrew term "Messiah." It must have been especially important to author and readers. But who would have been interested in the title except Jews? According to John 11:51f., Jesus' sacrifice leads to the gathering of those children of God who are scattered. Van Unnik views this gathering as a Messianic work. Thus the Fourth Gospel must have been written for Jews or Jewish Christians.[28] The term "Christ," meaning "the Anointed One," was "meaningless to Hellenistic churches and . . . there it prolonged its life as a proper name, that is to say: as a fossil. But that is clearly not the case in the Fourth Gospel; for John it is still full of life and can serve as the intelligible translation of a Hebrew word. This seems to me a strong indication that the gospel has something to do with Jews or Jewish Christians to whom the title 'the Anointed One' was important." [29]

In the feeding of the five thousand it is quite apparent that the Messiah concept is reinterpreted for Jews or Jewish Christians. The Galileans wanted to crown Jesus because they felt that he had celebrated with them the Messianic meal. The Fourth Gospel "does not say that Jesus did not want . . . to be the king of the Jews, but that he refused this manner of becoming king." Jesus is not the Messiah the way the Jews think of the Messiah. The Fourth Gospel makes a special point of it because Jesus' Messiahship "was the big issue between Jews and Christians. Pure Hellenists needed some other way of approach. 'That Jesus is the Christ,' *this Johannine phrase is a formula which has its roots in the Christian mission among the Jews.*" [30]

Van Unnik actually would not have to go so far as the Christian mission among the Jews of the Mediterranean to discover the origin of the phrase "That Jesus is the Christ." The Jerusalem apostles, that is, the first Christian community already had to come to grips with the problem that the Messiah was the concrete man Jesus of Nazareth who suffered on the cross. This involved a complete change in the picture of the Messiah. The Messiah had been "a figure of the *future* . . . the ideal, but imaginary deliverer . . . it never was a man of flesh and blood." [31] It may well be that the Fourth Gospel in its present form is a missionary document, as van Unnik contends: "*The purpose of the Fourth Gospel was to bring the visitors of a synagogue in the Diaspora (Jews and Godfearers) to belief in Jesus as the Messiah of Israel. . . .* It was a missionary book for the Jews." [32] But the nonecclesiastical interpretation goes much farther back. Regardless of whether or not Jesus thought of himself as Messiah, the distinction between his intention and the program of the Jewish ecclesiastics was at the root of his clash with the authorities. Having initiated in his work a new interpretation of Judaism, he gradually became the center of the reinterpretation of the Jewish ecclesiastical terminology among his followers.

The concepts used in the Fourth Gospel, insofar as they are rooted in Judaism, temple, resurrection, judgment, Lamb of God, and so forth, all had ecclesiastical significance. As the Fourth Gospel reinterprets them, they lose their ecclesiastical face value. Now Jesus' body, the body of a man, is the temple. Now Jesus is the resurrection and the judgment and—most important of all—the Messiah. Before we begin to introduce a nonreligious interpretation today, we will be well advised if we take note of the nonecclesiastical interpretation of the Fourth Gospel. It may be much more radical and relevant. Faith today must question the complacency of the ecclesiastical establishment as much as the supernaturalism of religion. Ecclesiasticism might even be a greater foe than religion. In fact, religion rightly understood might not be a real foe at all.

The author of the Fourth Gospel hardly wrote to satisfy himself.[33] The occasion for his work must have been his attempt to interpret Jesus to Jews—Hellenistic Jews—who were bound to the Jewish ecclesiastical establishment such as it was. It is probable that the basic material of the Fourth Gospel took shape in a Christian community in Judea and that the members of this community already had a controversy with "the Jews," that is, with those of the Jewish faith who did not accept Jesus as the Christ. After the Christian communities of Judea had been dispersed all over the Meriterranean world, the basic issue remained the same. In its present form the Fourth Gospel is thus best understood as "an appeal to those outside the Church, to win to the faith that Greek-speaking *Diaspora Judaism* to which the author now finds himself belonging as a result (we may surmise) of the greatest dispersion of all, which has swept from Judea Church and Synagogue alike." [34] Circumstances in the primitive church were such that nonecclesiastical interpretation became the very first step in communicating Jesus' history.

Nonecclesiastical interpretation in the Fourth Gospel is part and parcel of the historico-ontological hermeneutic. The ecclesiastical terminology of Judaism was in Jesus' day the matrix of meaning in which the Jewish community understood its primal experiences. Once the nonecclesiastical interpretation of the primitive church had reinterpreted the language of Judaism, it was a logical step to treat the Hellenistic quest for meaning in a similar way. Technically our experience today resembles the Hellenistic experience more than the Jewish quest. Temple, Lamb of God, judgment, etc., are images that relate specifically to the history of Israel. The present-day quest for meaning has a more general ontological base.

THE DIAKONIC DEED

To speak of a historico-ontological hermeneutic as a non-ecclesiastical interpretation of the Gospel means to focus only on the formal aspect of the historiography of the Fourth Gospel. We now turn to the problem of content.

We said that at the historical core of the initial interpretive process in Christianity lies the attempt of the primitive church to show that Jesus is the Messiah. From the historico-critical point of view, more important than the question of Jesus' Messianic self-consciousness—which is difficult to measure with historico-critical tools—is the impression his death created in the minds of his disciples. Regardless of *when* they began to think of him as the Messiah, they had to face the difficulty that the suffering of the Messiah entailed a readjustment of the Jewish concept of the Messiah. Some interpretation of the cross had to be given; otherwise, the disciples would have been completely at a loss.

It is impossible in brief to outline how the Fourth Gospel as a whole gradually became an interpretation of the cross.[35] A reference to one incident in the Gospel must suffice. At the beginning of the farewell discourses, that is, shortly before his trial and death, we find one more deed of Jesus which in the present composition of the Fourth Gospel is used as an interpretation of the cross. Jesus washed his disciples' feet. Knowing "that his hour had come to depart out of this world to the Father" (John 13:1) and "knowing that the Father had given all things

into his hands, and that he had come from God and was going
to God, [he] rose from supper, laid aside his garments, and girded
himself with a towel. Then he poured water into a basin, and
began to wash the disciples' feet, and to wipe them with the
towel with which he was girded." (John 13:3–5) At a supper
Jesus waits on his disciples "at table." The servant who waited
at table in Jesus' day was the *diakonos*. Now Jesus, the master,
waits on his disciples, but *in a new way*. In washing their feet he
performs the *new* diakonic deed.

If the Fourth Gospel would make no effort to find a larger
context for this deed, it would be less significant for our discussion. But Jesus is said to have done this deed *knowing that
the hour of his death had come, knowing that he was returning
to the Father*. The deed appears to be related to his going to the
Father. As it turns out, it becomes *the* interpretation of what his
going to the Father means. In its light the cross is seen as the
glorification of Jesus and simultaneously of God: "Now the Son
of man is glorified, and in him God is glorified." (John 13:31)
Glorification is manifestation of being, here the manifestation
of the very being of the Son of man and of God's being in him.
In fact, it is the diakonic deed that the Father appropriates as
his very own: "God will also glorify him in himself, and glorify
him at once." (John 13:32)

It is important to stress that Jesus' deed is a *new* diakonic
deed. That is, Jesus' *diakonia* does not necessarily express the
diakonia of everyday life. He took the forms of the world and
transformed them. The "apparent failure" of Jesus, in this diakonic context, becomes the characteristic embodiment of *agape*:
"A new commandment I give to you, that you love one another;
even as I have loved you." (John 13:34) The "as I loved you"
points to *agape* as costly love, *God's* kind of love, a love for which
a price was paid. Now we know why Jesus' life was directed to
the cross from the very beginning. Only in this radical diakonic
deed could costly love be embodied, could God be incarnate as
costly love. Without interpretation, however, the diakonic deed
would remain dumb. It would not be understood as a primordial
deed. Thus words accompany it.

We noted before that historical research in the life of Jesus always seems to center in on a basic historical datum, whether it be the cross or the Messianic consciousness or the resurrection. The question is: Which datum is truly central? The Fourth Gospel points to the cross: Jesus is the suffering Messiah. But history on the cross is mute.[36] At least it does not speak about God. Here language is needed for articulation, which in terms of the historico-ontological hermeneutic in the Fourth Gospel immediately introduces the problem of the primordial word.

THE POETIC WORD

Nonecclesiastical interpretation in the primitive church tried to do justice to the new factor that had entered Judaism in the death of Jesus of Nazareth. It regarded it as the suffering of the Messiah, but as the suffering of one who was intimately related to God. It took, however, an interpretation in a new language to grasp the essentially new factor introduced by Jesus' life. He is reported to have said: "It is the spirit that gives life . . . the words that I have spoken to you are spirit and life." (John 6:63) The words Jesus had spoken were remembered as *poetic* words in the sense of *creative* words. In the Greek form of the Apostles' Creed God is the ποιητὴς οὐρανοῦ καὶ γῆς, the Maker of heaven and earth. The creator is thus *the true poet*. The creativity which broke forth out of Jesus' words was also experienced as breaking forth out of his death—in the event of the resurrection. It is with reference to this creativity that we can appreciate the comment of Vincent van Gogh: "These spoken words, which, like a great prodigal lord, he did not even deign to write down, are one of the highest peaks, the highest in fact ever reached by art, which there becomes a creative force, a pure creative force." [37]

The art of creating life is, of course, the theme of the healing stories. Jesus says to the official from Capernaum whose son was at the point of death and who wanted Jesus to come and heal him: "Go; your son will live." (John 4:50) He tells the man thirty-eight years sick: "Rise, take up your pallet, and walk."

(John 5:8) The art of creating life is most dramatically portrayed as Jesus calls Lazarus—four days dead—out of the tomb: "Lazarus, come out." (John 11:43)

In the poetic word a transvaluation of reality as a whole takes place.[38] Water is now able to interpret Jesus' mission. To the Samaritan woman at the well he says: "Every one who drinks of this water will thirst again, but whoever drinks of the water that I shall give him will never thirst." (John 4:13f.) Bread is able to characterize Jesus' being: "I am the bread of life; he who comes to me shall not hunger." (John 6:35) Light is able to articulate his nature: "I am the light of the world; he who follows me will not walk in darkness, but will have the light of life." (John 8:12) The Fourth Gospel does not disregard nature and the categories in which man seeks to understand nature. The whole world is made to share in the interpretation of Jesus. Edwyn C. Hoskyns can thus say that the Fourth Gospel "far from evacuating the observable world of anything but secondary importance, establishes it as the place where men, living in the flesh, are confronted by the last things of God." It might even be "that in the final analysis the real and observable world, illuminated by the real and observable event of Jesus in the flesh, possesses in itself such immediate and direct witness to God that it is the witness of God to Himself." [39]

Jesus' word creatively inaugurates a new life. In his word men were confronted with a reality that fulfilled their primordial quest. Is there a word that can articulate man's primal experience? Hoskyns claims that "the Evangelist is pressed . . . from 'words' to word, and from a series of words to The Word." [40] Thus finally the evangelist sees the Father present in Jesus' word. In Jesus' healing of the man thirty-eight years sick, the Father himself is acting. In his word it becomes plain that Jesus is subservient to the Father: "The Son can do nothing of his own accord, but only what he sees the Father doing; for whatever he does, that the Son does likewise." (John 5:19) The creativity of the Father is reflected in the *poetic* word of the Son: "For as the Father raises the dead and gives them life, so also the Son gives life to whom he will." (John 5:21) In the poetic word of the raising of Lazarus it becomes manifest that there is a primordial word as articulated in John 1:1–3: "The word was God. He was in the beginning with God; all things were made through him." But the primordial word can never be known in the abstract. It is always "known" in the experience of Jesus' word as *poetic* word. Here Jesus' history fills the empty vessel of man's ontological quest. It fills it in such a way that being is felt in its dynamic creativity. Only then can the word "God" be added as its "name tag."

The most radical *poetic* word is spoken when Jesus says: "I and the Father are one." (John 10:30) This is not meant as a merely moral unity of will and purpose. It is a unity of being: "I and the Father *are* one." This unity is incarnate in the unity of action: "If I am not doing the works of my Father, then do not believe me; but if I do them, even though you do not believe me, believe the works, that you may know and understand that the Father is in me and I am in the Father." (John 10:37f.) The Father is present in Jesus. The Father *is* in Jesus. In Jesus' word and deed. The Father is also the Father beyond Jesus. But who he is is incarnate in the Son. In this way the Father *is* God. He is the true poet, and his Word is the primordial poem.[41]

THE NEW INTERPRETER

The methodology of the Fourth Gospel as a whole is directed by the work of the Interpreter Spirit. Man's attempt to come to grips with being ends in a puzzlement. As man tries to understand the history of Jesus he is no less at a loss, especially if he takes the cross into account. There is no way of avoiding the ontological and historical aporiae. Being and history as such are unable to give lasting meaning to Jesus' life. Only as they are joined in a creative act, not controlled by man's ingenuity, does meaning break forth. Hoskyns thus rightly stresses that the understanding of Jesus depends on God's self-interpretation: "The truth which Jesus *is* and *was* can be made known only by the Holy Spirit of God."[42] The Holy Spirit is God himself establishing a relationship with man after the crucifixion, uniting man's ontological quest with Jesus' history in a new understanding of life in the Word. Through the work of the Interpreter Spirit he who confronts Jesus' deed and word in the word of the witness can see, as it were, the inner history of the observable history. Holy Spirit is God's full presence in history as costly love—after cross and resurrection. It implies an ever-deepening grasp of God's being in the community of faith.

After the diakonic deed of the washing of the disciples' feet, Jesus refers to the Interpreter Spirit several times in his farewell discourses. In direct personal contact with Jesus the disciples had been unable to grasp fully everything he embodied. Even before the crucifixion had become for them a "mute" event, many of Jesus' words had proved to be mute. After Jesus' leaving however, the disciples were granted a more complete understanding. The Interpreter Spirit informed them of the true meaning of the cross and of Jesus' life.

Jesus says of the Spirit: "He will glorify me, for he will take what is mine and declare it to you." (John 16:14) The Spirit, uniting being and history in the Word, makes Jesus' meaning plain. The Spirit through Jesus interprets God to us and unites us with God as the meaning of our life. In articulate words, the words of the witness to Jesus, the Spirit confronts man with the subject of faith itself. God not only makes himself known in the word of the witness, but gives himself in this word. The words are spirit and life (John 6:33). The Word is God (John 1:1). The Word in the language of the witness mediates an encounter with God as the true subject of our hermeneutic concern. Here the "dialectic between language and its subject matter (*Sprache* and *Sache*)" [43] finds its proper focus: "God is His own interpreter and He will make it plain." [44]

In the Fourth Gospel the presence of the Spirit among men is tied to the resurrection (John 20:19–23). The resurrection, as it were, is the Johannine Pentecost. It stresses that the gift of the Spirit is not an additional "miracle" consummating other miraculous events, but the one act of interpretation that draws out the full meaning of Jesus' life and death. The gift of the Spirit is an act of Jesus himself. In bestowing the Spirit upon the disciples he says: "Receive the Holy Spirit. If you forgive the sins of any, they are forgiven; if you retain the sins of any, they are retained."

(John 20:22–23) These words immediately indicate that the central purpose of Jesus' life and death, the forgiveness of sins for the renewal of man's life in costly love, prevails beyond his death. Jesus' resurrection means that God's costly love shown in the forgiveness of sins lasts forever. The gift of the Spirit makes the lastingness of God's costly love concrete among men.

Systematic theology takes its starting point where the historical view of Jesus confronts us with an aporia, we said earlier. Now the mandate of its tasks becomes clearer. Systematic theology in its work depends on the Interpreter Spirit. It proceeds by acknowledging that it is the Spirit who creates understanding of Jesus' history. It presupposes the union of being and history in God's presence in Jesus. As regards the possibility of man's seeing God in Jesus today, it still depends on the Spirit. The methodological aspect of the work of the Spirit is his grounding of man's ontological and historical aporiae in God as the source of true being.

We began this chapter by pointing to the renewed interest of present-day theology in the Fourth Gospel. In view of the current hermeneutical concerns, we felt this to be a felicitous development because of the articulate hermeneutic of the Fourth Gospel. The Fourth Gospel, of course, represents only one strand of New Testament thought. Any present-day hermeneutic based on the Fourth Gospel will have to engage in dialogue with theologies whose hermeneutic is rooted in other strands of New Testament thought.

Perhaps the most creative statement of the present task of Protestant theology to appear in our decade thus far is Jürgen Moltmann's *Theologie der Hoffnung*.[45] It is strongly geared to hermeneutical concerns.[46] Its main thrust, however, is its attempt to restate the task of theology in terms of the eschatological dimension of the Christian life. Briefly referring to Moltmann's presuppositions, I wish to indicate which direction a dialogue with a theology rooted in a different strand of New Testament thought might take.

Moltmann apparently begins with a Pauline orientation. The God of St. Paul is "the God of hope" (Rom. 15:13), and his Christ is "the hope of glory." (Col. 1:27) In this context Moltmann lays down a fundamental working principle of his theology: "The present and the future, experience and hope contradict each other." The Christian hope is always directed toward that which is not as yet visible: "Now hope that is seen is not hope. For who hopes for what he sees? But if we hope for what we do not see, we wait for it in patience." (Rom. 8:24–25) On this basis Moltmann sets out to describe hope as "the foundation and motive of all theological thought" and to introduce "the eschatological perspective into the theological concepts of God's revelation, the resurrection, faith's mission and history." [47]

On this basis he also rejects the idea of God's and Christ's presence in history. God is not present as being. He is only present in his promise. The God of being is the God of Greek philosophy. The Logos of being was supposed to free man "for an eternal presence." And the concept of *parousia* represented for the Greeks the presence of being. When the primitive Christian community applied the concept to God and Christ, it became something radically different: the coming *parousia* of God and Christ, present only in the promise of the Gospel.[48]

Summarizing the difference between Christian eschatology and Greek philosophy, Moltmann states: "The true language of Christian eschatology is not the Greek Logos, but the *promise*, as it formed the speech, the hope, and the experience of Israel. Israel did not find God's truth in the Logos of the epiphany of the eternal presence, but in the word of promise founded on hope." [49] While it is true that there is a difference between the Greek Logos and Israel's concept of God's promise, one has to ask whether the New Testament as a whole sees as radical an antithesis here as Moltmann does. His emphasis on the Christian hope can only be welcomed in the present state of affairs in Protestant theology. But does the New Testament consistently speak in terms of a radical rupture between God's Word and the Logos of man?

It would seem that the Fourth Gospel states the relationship between God's *parousia* and God's Word in a way different from Moltmann. The Fourth Gospel relates both *parousia* and the Word to the Holy Spirit, God's New Interpreter. Through the Holy Spirit God is not only future, but also presence. To be sure, it is not a full presence or a consummate nearness. And it is certainly not a presence controlled by man. But in the Spirit God is truly Immanuel, God *with* us. In the context of his promise of the Spirit, Jesus tells his disciples: "I will not leave you desolate, I will come to you." (John 14:18) He comes in the Spirit and unites himself with the believer: "In that day you will know that I am in the Father, and you in me, and I in you." (John 14:20) In the same vein St. Paul can say that God "has put his seal upon us and given us his Spirit in our hearts as a guarantee." (II Cor. 1:22) The dialectic in which the Christian faith finds itself as regards the future is not one between not having at all and having everything, but of having in part and having fully. Thus St. Paul can say: "Now I know in part; then I shall understand fully, even as I have been fully understood. So faith, hope, love abide, these three; but the greatest of these is love." (I Cor. 13:12–13) The ultimate *parousia* is not eliminated. But man can have a foretaste of it in the Spirit.

It cannot be our task here to give a comprehensive overview of Moltmann's book. Suffice it to say that we regard it highly for its exegetical acumen and its unusual sensitivity for the dilemmas of modern man. What was necessary at this point was to lift out the problem that arises from using different biblical models in hermeneutical reflection. One thing is certain: we are at least able to engage in dialogue with Moltmann on this score because of our common biblical basis. The relationship of various biblical models is unfinished business in our book as it is in Protestant theology as a whole.[50] All we can hope for in our present situation is some agreement that this is the area where dialogue must begin. Moltmann's book is so refreshing because here a young theologian consistently tries to think through the theological task on the basis of the biblical word alone.

We wish to relate this word to the work of the Spirit in terms of the historico-ontological hermeneutic of the Fourth Gospel. The Spirit here overcomes man's lack of understanding not merely by giving man the promise of God's Word, but by addressing man's ontological and historical aporiae and transforming them in a new life with God's Word. God is not only proleptically in the Word. The Word is God.

To be sure, Moltmann is also aware of the significance of the

Spirit in theological reflection. In an essay which examines the position of Gerhard Ebeling, he writes that in the Spirit who gives life, the Spirit of hope, man is already aware of his authenticity and reconciliation with himself, although he still awaits its consummation.[51] His basic objection to Ebeling hinges on a different understanding of man's relationship to history. Moltmann claims: "The Gospel should not confront modern man who is battling for his future with a 'diakonic relationship to history,' a caring for and keeping of the origins and the tradition, but—in responsibility for the Messianic hope—with the process related to the future of truth as foreshadowed in the resurrection of Christ." Granted that man's redemption still awaits its consummation, and even granted that this might entail an Either-Or between a diakonic relationship to history (Ebeling's emphasis) and the responsibility for the future, does this exclude the experience of present truth in the Word?

If it is the case that in the Spirit we are already aware of the consummation, is it true that the *kerygma* is not Logos bringing truth, but only promise of still awaited future reality, as Moltmann argues? The Gospel indeed does not bring anxious man happy reassurance, but the struggle for obedience.[52] Even so, is not this struggle a wrestle with the *present* Word bringing man into truth, and a wrestle precisely because we are as yet unable to appropriate this truth more fully?

The Spirit makes us wait for what we do not have fully as yet. But we do meet God in the Word. And the Spirit *in the Word* gives us a foretaste of what it means that God will be "all in all." (I Cor. 15:28. King James)

⊰ IV ⊱

HISTORICO-ONTOLOGICAL
HERMENEUTIC TODAY

*Sleeps a song in every thing
That is dreaming still unheard.
And the world begins to sing
If you find the magic word.*[1]

JOSEPH VON EICHENDORFF

IN the present Protestant debate about hermeneutic[2] we observe two tendencies. On the one hand, there is a trend toward an ontologically oriented hermeneutic represented by Heinrich Ott's use of the later Heidegger.[3] Unfortunately Ott does not explore thoroughly enough the historical dimension of hermeneutic. On the other hand, the more historical concern in hermeneutic, represented by Ernst Fuchs and Gerhard Ebeling, is not sufficiently joined to the ontological quest. At least this is the impression one gets from their essays in *The New Hermeneutic,* edited by James M. Robinson and John B. Cobb, Jr. If we turn to the *corpus* of Fuchs' and Ebeling's writings, the point has to be modified. Even so, the historical and ontological aspects of hermeneutic are not so systematically joined as they might be in terms of Fuchs' and Ebeling's hermeneutical intention.

Our examination of the hermeneutic of the Fourth Gospel leads us to ask whether the historical and ontological concerns could not be more closely related in the contemporary debate. A unique historical event has been brought to bear on the ontological aporia. But only in the light of categories and concepts developed in the effort to come to grips with the ontological aporia does the historical event take on meaning.

To speak of meaning means to articulate a dimension even more fundamental than the ontological and the historical as such. Historical data in themselves are as silent as being. Historical events become history for us, and being puzzles us because we want to understand. We want to find some union between historical events and being. History and ontology here revert to hermeneutic.

We do not intend to identify all of theology with hermeneutic. All we wish to ascertain in the hermeneutic of God is the primal movement of thought that lies at the basis of theological knowledge. The historico-ontological hermeneutic related to the word "God" for us belongs primarily to an introduction to systematic theology.

THE NEW HERMENEUTIC AND THE ONTOLOGY OF LANGUAGE

In view of the recent developments in systematic theology, it is understandable that the hermeneutical problem as a specific issue is returning to the foreground of the theological debate. After the historical issue had again been stressed in the new quest of the historical Jesus and ontology had been re-introduced as a context for the interpretation of the Christian faith, the actual process of thought that imposes upon man the historical and ontological concerns once more became a challenging subject of inquiry. In *The New Hermeneutic* this challenge has found a sharp focus.

James M. Robinson, in "Hermeneutic Since Barth," his introductory essay in *The New Hermeneutic*, notes that from the eighteenth century to recent times hermeneutic in theology has been regarded as the theory of exegesis, while exegesis itself has been understood as the practice of interpretation and distinguished from criticism, the historical reconstruction of the text. It was only when Wilhelm Dilthey's distinction of the difference between explaining occurrences in nature and interpreting historical events became more widely appreciated that hermeneutic began to cover a more comprehensive concern. For the sake of clarity in distinctions Robinson reserves the term "hermeneutics" (with the *s*) for the older ap-

proach and uses "hermeneutic" (without the *s*) for the trend inaugurated by Dilthey: "The new hermeneutic began to emerge in a
recognition of the superficiality of hermeneutics, and hence in an
intentional distinction of its deeper concern for understanding from
that of hermeneutics." [4] This new trend found a strong spokesman
in Rudolf Bultmann. But Robinson cautions as regards Bultmann's
view: "Its implication of getting behind the words to the existence
objectifying itself in them calls to attention both the depth and the
limitation characteristic of this first step toward a new hermeneutic." [5] What emerges as the new hermeneutic today is thus supposed to lead beyond the findings of Bultmann and his scheme of
existentialist demythologizing. In fact, the new hermeneutic is more
than simply "understanding." It is an interpretation of reality as
a whole. In the following paragraphs we will try to trace what we
consider the basic views of the new hermeneutic. But we wish to
stress once more that we shall limit our own hermeneutic to the
elementary components of the understanding of God.

The step beyond Bultmann to a new hermeneutic Robinson
finds completed in Fuchs and Ebeling. The hermeneutical point
of reference is no longer existence, but language: "It is a central
recognition of the new hermeneutic that language itself says what
is invisibly taking place in the life of a culture." *Man is no longer
the central hermeneutical concern:* "It is indeed not man at all who
is ex-pressing himself in language. Rather it is language itself that
speaks." If it is not man who expresses himself in language, one
might think that in speaking it is *only* language that expresses itself. But this is not the case: "The subject matter of which language
speaks is primarily being. . . . In this way language is located at
the center of man's nature, rather than being regarded primarily as
an objectification of an otherwise authentic self-understanding. For
man's nature is defined as linguistic, in that his role is to re-speak,
to re-spond, to an-swer, the call of being." [6] Thus the new hermeneutic moves away from an anthropocentric existentialism. It tries
to interpret the nature of man in the light of an ontology of language. This is a significant shift. But does it press the ontological
issue far enough?

According to Robinson, Martin Heidegger's recent views on
the nature of language have provided the representatives of the

new hermeneutic with the concepts that made them explore possible new approaches to theology. It is especially Ernst Fuchs who has appreciated "Heidegger's lament about inauthentic language as an indirect witness to true language, somewhat as the law is related to the gospel." Inauthentic language is best understood if one realizes that it is "only the perversion of authentic language." There is, of course, a difference between what the philosopher and the theologian define as authentic language. "Fuchs finds authentic language in Jesus' language of love, and thus moves from Heidegger into a 'christological understanding of language.' " [7] Here a new view of language emerges that is characterized as christological. What is it, however, that distinguishes Jesus' language of love from other languages? If one speaks of the *christo*logical interpretation of love, one willy-nilly introduces a *theo*logical factor. Here a whole complex of issues looms that needs careful examination.

As noted before, Robinson presents the new hermeneutic in such a way that it appears as a real advance in theological thought. The advance seems to center in the concept of the *hermeneutical principle*. This concept demands that we no longer try to find meaning in ourselves but in the text: "Here one can see interpretation taking place less as 'understanding' than as 'language,' in that the text interprets itself by what it has to say about us." In order for this to happen a translation has to take place, a transporting of the text into our lives: "Thus hermeneutic as translation stands in contrast to the Schleiermacher-Dilthey hermeneutic of becoming 'contemporary' with the author—reliving his experience." [8]

It is necessary at this point to ask whether or not the emphasis on *hermeneutic as language* is successful in articulating important elements of the hermeneutical process. Does it make its presuppositions explicit in an adequate way? What does it mean that there is also a language of love?

Ernst Fuchs makes a crucial hermeneutical affirmation in his essay "The New Testament and the Hermeneutical Problem" when he says: "*Now let one replace the word 'love' with the word 'God.' Then one has understood that faith in God is the most natural thing that there can be.* And it readily makes sense to our practical reason." [9] Hermeneutically one would like to know: Why should the replacement of the word "love" by the word "God" make sense to our practical reason? What is the practical reason in which the word "God" seems somehow rooted with meaning *via* the word "love"? Is "love" the more basic reality that can make sense of the word "God"?

The new hermeneutic, at least as represented in the volume under consideration, does not sufficiently articulate its prejudgments. As a hermeneutician Fuchs is obligated to reveal the nature of his court of appeal. Only in this way might we be able to know *by what question the new hermeneutic is guided* in its procedure.[10] We noted before that the *christo*logical understanding of language willy-nilly implies a *theo*logical factor. Christology is concerned with Jesus in relationship to God. As long as one does not make this fact explicit hermeneutically, one is apt to beg the question.

In Fuchs we are confronted with a strange tension between the christological interpretation of language and practical reason, which is supposed to be able to make sense of the language of love. How are these two poles related? Is it a christological view of language that guides the interpretation of the new hermeneutic or is it practical reason? Or both?

The reorientation of the hermeneutical perspective in the new hermeneutic is obvious: it is not so much that man in his self-understanding interprets the text as that the text interprets man. But it is impossible to say that understanding is a one-way affair: from text to man. If in a hermeneutic of the word "God" we ask how God can be understood, we cannot exclude the analysis of man's involvement. What do the ontological and historical aporiae contribute to the understanding of God? Here at least *The New Hermeneutic* keeps us in suspense.

Appealing to the conviction of the German philosopher Gadamer that man's being consists more in his prejudgments than in his judgments, Robinson comments that the "historic 'prejudice' with which our experience is loaded is primarily our language."[11] While this clarifies the issue in general, it still leaves open the question of what the specific prejudice is with which a word of our language, the word "God," might be loaded. John B. Cobb clarifies the discussion in his evaluation of the debate by singling out the issue of the significance of presuppositions in coming to grips with hermeneutic. There are different sets of presuppositions, on grounds of which one will arrive at different results. Or, in John Cobb's words: "Different views of faith . . . lead to different practice of hermeneutic." [12] It is regrettable that in his "Response to the American Discussion" [13] Fuchs disregards this critique almost completely. Instead he turns to the problem of preaching.

In reaction to the American evaluation by Wilder and Cobb, Fuchs asserts that "Amos Wilder and John Cobb almost deliberately overlook the fact that Ebeling's and my own effort at hermeneutical reflection, materially speaking, is concerned with how the text, seen as a merely historical source, can again become the text of preaching." Answering his own question, he tries to clarify the significance of the new hermeneutic: "But why 'new' hermeneutic? Answer: Precisely for the sake of the ancient hermeneutical problem as to how it is that preaching should use specifically the Bible as its text. Within dogmatics the question appears as follows: Why does Christian faith rest upon proclamation? Seen from a hermeneutical point of view dogmatics then becomes quite consciously a doctrine of the word of God." Proclamation indeed is the goal of every hermeneutical effort in theology. But to point to proclamation without seeking to clarify the matter of presuppositions hardly does justice to the hermeneutical mandate. Hermeneutically one must articulate the *components* of the translation of a text. This demands that one consider man's aporiae. In what way does man become involved in the subject of the text?

Fuchs uses the word "God" over and over again. For one example: "*Without God one does not understand a believer.* One must understand what he finds in God, why he holds to God. Then one understands the believer and his faith." [14] But the context contains no interpretation as to how the word "God" might be a bridge from the text to man's aporia. Robinson observes that for Fuchs "the confrontation with our need . . . reveals what we mean by the term God." [15] But this does not help us much further, since the hermeneutical aspect of the need is not qualified.

The principal emphasis of Fuchs is that the New Testament teaches "the hermeneutic of faith—in brief, the language of faith—and it encourages us to try out this language ourselves, so that we may become familiar with—God." [16] *Why* with—God? It is only at the point where Fuchs says that love interprets the word "God," an instance we have appealed to before, that we are confronted with the task any hermeneutic must consider primary: the articulation of its prejudgments. In his reaction to the American discussion, Fuchs returns to the significance of the word "love" for his hermeneutic of God: "Is God love, as the New Testament says (I John 4:16)? That is decided by the word, whether at the right time and place the word of love, its Yes, is possible or is denied." [17] In our opinion Fuchs does not press far enough. Does the word "love" as such suffice to interpret the word "God"? The hermeneutical experience of man at this point seems more complex.

It would make for a sharper focus of the new hermeneutic if it could see the significance of the new quest of God and would work on a hermeneutic of God rather than a hermeneutic of faith. What Fuchs seems to be seeking an answer for is the question of God. But it is not articulated as a distinct question that guides the theological endeavor. On Fuchs' grounds, however, there appears to be the possibility of making it *the guiding question.*[18] Fuchs points to language if one asks what the word "God" means. For language is the sphere where our life can be brought to the light of truth. But it seems that we would misunderstand Fuchs if we were to assume that language as such is for him the ultimate court of appeal. The sphere of language is encompassed by the sphere of love: "*The language of man belongs in the sphere of love.*" [19] I take this to mean that Fuchs appeals to *a sphere in which language is rooted.* In other words, there is an *ontology of language.*

Initially the word "love" was supposed to illumine the word "God." Now it is the sphere of love that is supposed to illumine language. *The sequence from love to word* is perhaps expressed in the following: "A word can have the characteristic—which is what first makes it 'word'—that, in contrast to nothing, being happens for us. When we are met with love, then love, as being, comes in the word and into language, and it remains there, too. If love goes, the word goes." As love moves into language there is a "language gain." The gain of language through love has its source in Jesus' preaching.[20] Interestingly enough, here again Fuchs has immediately moved away from the ontology of language to its historical dimension. We can hardly do more than observe the tension. It might have clarified the problem if at some point Fuchs would have analysed the relationship between "being" and the "love" of which he speaks. What ontological structure is to be found in a love so closely related to being?

In the end, Fuchs has carefully argued through the historical dimension of love. But as regards the relationship of love to practical reason we remain on uncertain ground. Perhaps this has something to do with Fuchs' principal anthropological conviction "that our existence as men is constituted . . . by 'linguisticality'." [21] Focusing on the linguisticality of faith, Fuchs asks: "Is that the 'meaning' of the word of God?" and *not*: Is that the meaning of the word "God"? The difference between the new hermeneutic and our position lies here. Fuchs considers hermeneutic in theology as "nothing else than the 'doctrine of the word of God' (Ebeling), faith's doctrine of language." [22] By contrast, in our view, hermeneutic in theology must begin with an interpretation of the word "God." Not in any narrow sense, but in full realization that every concept of theology, every theological assertion, grows out of the elementary understanding of God. Ebeling himself understands the significance of the word "God" quite well when he says: "The truth of every utterance of faith depends on one thing, that God is. . . . Faith, wherever it speaks, and in all that it says and confesses . . . is faith in God and the unfolding of this sole truth of faith." [23] But this insight does not become dominant in his essay on hermeneutic.

The first step in discussing the hermeneutic of theological language must be the examination of the ontological roots of the word "God." What Paul Tillich says as regards logical positivism also pertains to the concern of the new hermeneutic in theological language: "There is always at least one problem about which logical positivism, like all semantic philosophies, must make a decision. What is the relation of signs, symbols, or logical operations to reality? Every answer to this question says something about the structure of being. It is ontological. And a philosophy which is so radically critical of all other philosophies should be sufficiently self-critical to see and to reveal its own ontological assumptions." [24] Occasionally in the new hermeneutic its prejudgments, its ontological assumptions, become visible. But the sphere of love to which

language is supposed to belong, according to Fuchs, is never explicitly related to the ontological query.

It would be preposterous to try to do for the new hermeneutic
what it itself does not do. But it was necessary to uncover its *lack
of hermeneutical explicitness*. Language contains prejudgments as
to what reality is like.[25] It is the first hermeneutical step to show
how language is related to reality. Theology must inquire whether
or not language contains a prejudgment concerning God. Gerhard
Ebeling thinks that "the verbal statement must always be coupled
with a corresponding relation to reality." Hermeneutic *"addresses
itself directly to the reality* that comes to understanding through the
word." We would like to know what all this means as regards the
word "God," especially since Ebeling claims that only "where word
has already taken place can word take place." [26] What does this say
about the hermeneutical circle once the word "God" becomes
dominant?

One of the striking phenomena on the present theological
scene is the parallelism between the interest of the new hermeneutic
in language and the concern for linguistic philosophy in British
and American theology. It is a challenging task for our theological
generation to try to unite the two trends. In the context of our
discussion we wish to point out only one significant possibility. It
is one of the strong points of Frederick Ferré's position in *Language,
Logic and God* that he sees the nexus between language and ontology. He frankly acknowledges the ultimate outcome of linguistic
analysis in theology: "There seems no escape from the conclusion
that the intended semantic reference of theological discourse is to
'metaphysical fact' of some kind." [27] This fact is "a concept which
plays a key role within the system, without which the system would
founder." For Ferré this implies a peculiar quality of theological
language: "To say that theological discourse refers to 'metaphysical
fact' is equivalent to asserting that theological language *on its
semantic dimension* functions as metaphysical language." [28]

For theological linguistics what Ferré reveals as his final position might be sufficient, but hermeneutically it leads us only to
beginnings: "Theological speech projects a model of immense

responsive significance, drawn from 'the facts,' as the key to its conceptual synthesis. . . . For Christianity . . . the conceptual model consists in the creative, self-giving, personal love of Jesus Christ. In this model is found the only literal meaning which these terms, like 'creative,' 'personal,' and 'love,' can have in the Christian vocabulary. All the concepts of the Christian are organized and synthesized in relation to this model." In Ferré I find no explicit concern for the historical dilemma which the talk about the model of self-giving might presuppose, and how it might mesh with the inability of man to come to grips with his encounter with being. What appears to Ferré in his theological linguistics as a "final consideration" is the elementary one for the hermeneutic of God: "The metaphysician and the theologian-as-metaphysician insist that their syntheses have *ontological* bearing. . . . In what respect can theological statements claim to be *true* to reality?" [29]

For the hermeneutic of God the elementary question explicitly formulated is: What is the ontological status of the word "God" as part of man's language? To relate the word "God" immediately to love—as Fuchs does in his essay in *The New Hermeneutic*—might mean to skip the primary hermeneutical reflection. Perhaps Fuchs in making the equation is too much influenced by his christological understanding of language.[30] The primal hermeneutical task in theology is the bridging of the gap between the christological interpretation of language and such prejudgments contained in man's language as are related to God. In focusing on the word "God," the intention of the new hermeneutic might become more lucid. Hermeneutic as conceived of by Ebeling and Fuchs in *The New Hermeneutic* develops too quickly into too broad an enterprise. Why should theology as a whole be regarded as a hermeneutic? Is it not sufficient to regard hermeneutic as the first step in theological prolegomena? Here, at least, we shall limit it to this area.

THE NEW HERMENEUTIC AND HISTORY

The turn toward language is to a certain extent a by-product of a new turn toward the historical Jesus. As James M. Robinson sees it the term "kerygma," central in Bultmann's demythologizing program, has almost disappeared from the vocabulary of the new hermeneutic: "If Bultmann can say that Jesus rose into the kerygma, Fuchs and Ebeling would say that the word event inaugurated by Jesus' word happens today in the church's proclamation. Thus the term 'kerygma'—which has functioned to separate the church's proclamation from the historical Jesus—tends to pass out of the vocabulary of the new hermeneutic, and to be explained and replaced by the term language event or word event in which Jesus' and the church's proclamation belong together." [31] It thus becomes a crucial problem to discover what is gained by replacing concern for the kerygma with Jesus' word.

According to Robinson, the proponents of the new hermeneutic hope by way of the language event or word event to bridge the gap between the historical Jesus and the present situation of the church as well as between the various branches of theology, especially between historical and systematic theology: "If the new hermeneutic thus proposes to bridge the gulf between historical and systematic theology in terms of a recurrent event of language that moves from Jesus' word to that of the preacher, then the new hermeneutic has become in fact a new understanding of theological scholarship as a whole." [32] While no theologian would wish to doubt the value of a project that seeks to unite the *disjecta membra* of present-day theology, one has to assess its foundations carefully. Perhaps they have been laid well in one area, but not in another.

What is clear is that the new hermeneutic wishes to turn from demythologizing *to Jesus and the meaning of his word*. Robinson describes the whole endeavor as the "translation of meaning in the recurring event of language," [33] uniting the historical datum of Jesus' word with the present moment of preaching. The relationship between Jesus' language and its subject matter as it relates to the present moment is the focus of the new hermeneutic. In this respect the foundations have been well laid. It is the "dialectic between language and subject matter (*Sprache* and *Sache*) rather than that between mythological language and the existential self-understanding it objectifies, which designates the point at which the hermeneutical discussion in Germany now stands." [34] The new hermeneutic has carefully articulated the historical dimension of hermeneutic in theology. But it has not made it quite as clear how the ontological dimension is fused with the historical dimension of Jesus' language.

There is another complication. The new hermeneutic approaches Jesus' language under the guidance of a specific question. Jesus' historical word depends in part on what the interpreter expects of it. As I understand it, the leading question for Ernst Fuchs is the question of faith. According to Fuchs, Jesus formulated his word in such a way that *"the hearer has something to hold to in the future also, as if a model of faith were given him to take along. Of course Jesus himself later entered with his person into this position and as the crucified became the model of faith.* But we can still detect that this was earlier so decidedly the case with regard to the most characteristic words of Jesus that other persons could readily create new and similar sayings. For this reason the question of authenticity is not so important as one supposes. It is enough that a saying becomes recognizable as a model of faith, so that we have a right to regard the saying as characteristic for Jesus." [35] What is faith? Is it really true that the New Testament is primarily interested in Jesus as *the model of faith?* What about Jesus' relationship to God? Could not this be made the center of the guiding question? Moreover, how is it possible that man can create sayings *similar to Jesus' sayings?* What creative power is here implied or presupposed?

The historical dimension of the new hermeneutic proves still too isolated from the primal hermeneutical endeavor. It is articulated without a full grasp of the interpenetration of the ontological and historical aporiae. Once again, we would wish that Robinson's and Cobb's *The New Hermeneutic* had not made hermeneutic such an all-embracing enterprise. Without endangering the present-day theological endeavor, hermeneutic might well be limited to the examination and development of the method of understanding.

HISTORY AND ONTOLOGY

If one asks the question of the hermeneutic of the word "God," the issues of systematic theology boil down to two points. Man develops his self-understanding in a constant debate with his en-

vironment. In his wrestle with his Whence and Whither he becomes aware of his quest for a primordially meaningful word. He
senses that he is response-able to this word, but he deflects this
awareness, ignoring the word's claim. He cannot make full sense of
life. Finally, a datum of history, the cross, confronts him in his
aporia. At this point only one question becomes important for the
clarification of man's nature and destiny: Will man find the meaning he seeks in the encounter between God's incarnate Word and
his quest for the primordial Word?

We dare not simplify the complex issues that have been
raised in the recent hermeneutical debate of Protestantism. But a
brief review of its background will show that the remaining unsolved
problems are relatively few and clearly to be seen. In the situation
in which Bultmann confronted the hermeneutical claim, he was
forced to concern himself with myth in the New Testament. The
demythologization he aspired to achieve already contained a reduction of a multiplicity of historical and ontological issues. The core
of his proposal was the invitation to appropriate two "data": cross
and resurrection. He believed that by relating both to man's existence he could "convince" man that to re-experience them meant
to experience the transition from inauthentic to authentic life.

While Bultmann related the transition very well to the historical event of the proclamation of the *kerygma* in the primitive
church,[36] on the one hand, and to man's capacities, on the other, it
never became quite clear whether God himself provided any ontological foundation for the transition from inauthentic to authentic
existence.[37] Love was to be regarded "from the outset [as] an ontological possibility of human existence of which man dimly knows,"
but not as an ontological reality of human existence.[38] Love enters
the picture as a determination of man's resolve. To speak of love
merely as an ontological possibility seems to rule out love as ontological actuality in God as well as in man. For Bultmann God was still
a God who acts. But what was the basis for God's action? It almost
seemed that God had become captive to the articulation of the
words of the *kerygma* or the proclamation as Bultmann had defined it.

Tillich's principally ontological approach was a distinct clarification over that of Bultmann. By stressing deliteralizing instead of

demythologizing, Tillich was able to get closer to the root of the hermeneutical claim. It was surprising that Tillich had to state the obvious: no religious word can be taken literally. It always refers to a more primary reality, a reality that can only be expressed symbolically. But while the ontological foundation of man's understanding in God became the center of Tillich's hermeneutic, the historical dimension of the Christian faith began to fade. What appeared important to Tillich was the essential unity of man with the Logos structure of his being. The incarnate Word seemed to be less significant.

Enters at this point a new hermeneutic. It claims that the thing that really matters is the word of Jesus. The historical dimension of a theological hermeneutic seems sharply focused. What more can be done? Hermeneutically we are driven to examine, as it were, the "nuclear structure" of theology. Can we "split the hermeneutical atom?" What are its smallest particles? In our perspective they are found in the ontological structure of the history so well focused in the new hermeneutic. The practical reason according to which, in Fuchs' language, love makes sense to man might contain a pre-awareness of love that drives man to long for its full manifestation. What prejudgment is contained in language as it uses the word "love"? It may well be that the pre-awareness of love is a "John the Baptist" that prepares the way of the Lord—precisely in its lack of understanding costly love. John the Baptist also was caught in a puzzlement: "Are you he who is to come, or shall we look for another?" (Matt. 11:3) His lack of understanding, his puzzlement, contained a pre-awareness. Otherwise he would not have asked his question.

The word "love" might make sense once we have understood that man's longing to be is fulfilled in the experience of costly love, the costly love of the cross. Love might make sense as that which truly is. In the word that interprets the cross as costly love we meet the meaning of the word "God" as we simultaneously become conscious of our pre-awareness of love. The present moment has the same content as the word that witnesses to Jesus' costly love.

Learning from the new quest of God that it is necessary to center in on the word "God," the new hermeneutic could perhaps clarify its basic purpose and avoid becoming too broad an undertaking.[39] And if the new quest of God learns to look for an understanding of God's being in the *language of love,* it might find the sufficient framework for its search. In joining the new hermeneutic with the new quest of God, it might also become evident that we do not need Heidegger's language to interpret God.[40] Christianity is a language event that can find meaning in the creativity of its own primal language as found in the New Testament.

GOD'S WORDPRESENCE

Our examination of the new hermeneutic resulted in the understanding that it is necessary to ascertain some order of hermeneutical reflection. What is the primary hermeneutical inquiry of the Christian faith? We noted earlier that in the Fourth Gospel the hermeneutic of God focuses initially on the Passion story. From the aporia in the face of the cross, man's lack of understanding moves to the words of Jesus and from there to their ontological roots. We thus spoke of a *historico*-ontological hermeneutic. It is from history that we move toward ontology. The interplay between history and ontology informs the story of Jesus with meaning—God acting as his own interpreter in the Spirit, and the history of Jesus always initiating the interplay.

In the Fourth Gospel the words and signs of Jesus are an interpretation of the aporia of the cross. Without words, even the signs that want to interpret the cross would be mute. One only has to think of the frequent "misunderstandings" of the signs by the disciples. We stressed the creative character of Jesus' words: "The words that I have spoken to you are spirit and life." (John 6:63) They create a constellation of understanding God that did not exist before. But his words do not operate in a vacuum of language. Jesus speaks to the Jews presupposing that they might have God's word abiding in them. He tells them: "You do not have his word abiding in you." (John 5:38) As one tries to pry open the meaning of this saying, one begins to grasp why the words in Jesus' discourses and his signs are insufficient for a full understanding of the structure of his communication. It was therefore necessary that the discourses and signs receive a preface in the prologue.

All of Jesus' words are rooted in the primordial Word. If man does not refuse the presence of this Word within him when he is confronted with Jesus' words, he is able to understand Jesus. If he does not see that his quest for the primordial Word is his search for God's Word, he will also reject Jesus of Nazareth. Our claim here is based on our previous hermeneutical decision. The Fourth Gospel affirms that man's being co-inheres in the primordial Word. That man can quest for a word articulating his origin and destiny is due to the overpowering presence of the Word itself. In this Word he is met by the ultimately real he is longing for and which he calls "God." Thus the prologue can say: "In the beginning was the Word . . . and the Word was God." (John 1:1)

This is a judgment made in the light of what the author of the Fourth Gospel believed to be the answer to the quest for the primordial Word. The fulfillment of this quest in the cross and in Jesus' life does not change. The shape of Jesus' being remains the same. What changes is the manner in which man appropriates it. Confronted with the cross, man today is also challenged to reorient his quest for the ultimately real. But what sense can present-day man find in the cross?

The understanding of God depends on the hermeneutical circle between man's quest for the primordial Word and the cross. Jesus' words unite the primordial Word and the cross in a texture of meaning. In the primordial Word God himself is present as he was present in Jesus. His presence with man is Wordpresence. The embodiment of God's Wordpresence in the incarnation is the fulfillment of man's quest for the presence of meaning in his life. Understanding in this respect is tied to certain texts, the texts of the Bible. After the incarnation God's Wordpresence became concrete once more in the biblical word. Thus we discern three modes of God's Wordpresence: (1) God's primordial Wordpresence in the structure of man's being; (2) God's incarnate Wordpresence in Jesus; and (3) God's biblical Wordpresence.

The cross involved a deed. Jesus' words in the context of his ministry interpret the cross, so that it is revealed as a *deed-word*. And in understanding Jesus' words, we experience God's Wordpresence as a *word-deed*. Jesus embodied the unity of word and deed. In him they do not fall apart as two different things. His deed is word. And his word is always a deed. *Faust* wants to improve on John 1:1 and claims: In the beginning was the deed! [41] But there is no need to improve on John 1:1, for its understanding of the Word includes the deed-character of the Word; it is *God's* Word.

With the concept of God's primordial Wordpresence we wish to point to the mystery that God is always present to man. Earlier we described man's being as self-dual. Apparently Gerhard Ebeling too wishes to retain a duality in the new hermeneutic: "Word is therefore rightly understood only when it is viewed as an event which—like love—involves at least two." [42] He works with a hermeneutical circle similar to the one we have outlined: "That Christian faith has adopted the hermeneutical approach is indeed identical with its having assented to the possibility and necessity of theology. And that again was expressed in its asserting an association between the Biblical concept of the word of God and the Logos concept of Greek philosophy." [43] In the contemporary situation the same hermeneutical circle is operative as in the New Testament text. But it calls for a distinctly contemporary interpretation. In order to clarify the present-day implications of our concept of God's Wordpresence, we briefly review Ebeling's presuppositions as a foil.

Ebeling suggests that it is language as such which today expresses man's quest of God. He sees that the answer to man's question cannot avoid the affirmation that *God is*. He even attempts to specify the nature of God's being: "To say that *God is* can only mean that we do have a future." Presupposed is, of course, that "the burning task of interpretation includes the question what 'God' really means." But present-day theology must realize that it is confronted with a unique situation in this respect: "To-day we face the question how, without the evidence of proofs of God's existence, and without the presupposition of a religious need for God, we may speak of God, and speak, moreover, in a way that is both understandable and relevant." [44]

At this point Ebeling's approach becomes especially important for the new quest of God. Reflecting on the meaning of the word "God," he says: "What the word 'God' means can in the first instance only be expressed as a question, namely, as a pointer to the radical questionableness which touches every man. . . . Whatever one's judgment about the question of God, it is clear that man is at

least not his own creator, but has been thrown into existence without being given any choice of time or place or circumstances." [45] Elsewhere Ebeling makes the same point: "God is experienced as a question. In the context of the reality that encounters me God encounters me as the questionableness of that encountering reality." Man's quest of God is answered in a word-event in which God shares human reality: "Despite all the doubts that have to be raised against the early church's Logos doctrine, it is definitely right in its grasp of this: that 'word' is what links and binds God and our reality." It is a linguistic event in which God draws near and in which we know God.[46]

With our concept of Wordpresence we wish to indicate in contrast to Ebeling that the word-event of the understanding of God is tied to the structure of the Word in which God already has reached man before the word of proclamation reaches him. Man is not confronted merely with a relative historical word of an individual man who happens to be talking about God.[47] Rather, in the historical word he is asked to remember his very being in the Word.

POETIC PROCLAMATION

The examination of the nucleus of hermeneutic in theology is not an end in itself.[48] Like all theological work it is directed toward communication which finds its focus in proclamation. Ebeling reflects on the relationship between proclamation and biblical texts and concludes that these texts as such do not seek to be proclaimed: "Rather it is God's word that is to be proclaimed, and that is one single word, but not words of God, not a variety of different texts." [49] From our perspective we can agree that the biblical texts do not seek to be sermon texts. They intend to mediate God's Wordpresence. The Old Testament witnesses to the Wordpresence of God the Creator; the New Testament, to God's incarnate Wordpresence. Even so, their witness, which seeks to mediate God's Wordpresence, has to be "rekindled" time and again. Thus the present moment has to be related to the past, to the witness of Holy Scripture. Or, in Ebeling's words: "Proclamation that has taken place is to become proclamation that takes place.

This transition from text to sermon is a transition from Scripture to the spoken word." [50]

Earlier we outlined the hermeneutic of the Fourth Gospel. We stated that we do not consider the Fourth Gospel the only model of theological thought. But we also stressed its unusual capacity for giving direction to present-day systematic theology because of its hermeneutical explicitness. All we wish to show now is that proclamation or preaching at its core is an attempt to recapture the hermeneutical structure of the historico-ontological method.

(1) Proclamation presupposes man's awareness of being and his aporia in the face of being. The new quest of God suggests that man's experience of his lack of understanding God be interpreted in relation to the primordial structure of his being. The articulation of the hermeneutical puzzlement that proclamation is faced with, however, does not go beyond the formal aspect of the problem.

(2) As regards content, proclamation takes its cue from Jesus' preaching. In the Fourth Gospel he uses the materials available in human experience in order to interpret his deeds, especially his deed on the cross. He apparently trusted their capacity to serve as interpretive material for his deed. For example, he used the foot-washing custom of his environment to embody the meaning of his life. It was not the footwashing as such that proclaimed. It was his word, but his word tied to the image of the footwashing.

(3) Jesus' preaching was poetic proclamation.[51] He creatively reshaped reality by his deed. He sensed the "song" that lies dormant in reality as a whole. All things could "sing" meaning into life if he only touched them with the proper word. In Jesus' interpretation footwashing did not remain trite, everyday footwashing, but became a *new* diakonic deed. For God himself communed with man through this deed in order to be present in Jesus' word. In footwashing God shared himself as *costly love*. In the poetic proclamation of this deed human reality was shaped anew. Preaching today must search for those images which most creatively can convey God's *waiting on man* and articulate it distinctly. We do not consider it our task to produce a recipe for creating these images. They must be found in the creative encounter with reality by the one who proclaims. It must be a personal discovery. What we can do in terms of principle is to point out that the creative encounter with

reality must be related to the Scriptures for proclamation to take place.

(4) Poetic, that is, creative, images of proclamation are able to draw upon a resource in the structure of reality that is not completely without parallel in other realms of communications.[52] Enid Welsford has spoken of this resource with respect to the fool in her book *The Fool:* [53] "Whenever the clown baffles the policeman, whenever the fool makes the sage look silly, whenever the acrobat defeats the machine, there is a sudden sense of pressure relieved, of a birth of new joy and freedom." This birth of new joy and freedom is a creative act, a poetic act, so that "one begins to discern a possibility that belief in the relationship between the poet, the seer and the fool may be more than an antiquated superstition. . . ." In fact, the birth of new joy and freedom is a genuine experience "as available in the twentieth century as in the so-called Dark Ages—the experience, namely, of two kinds of wisdom: the wisdom of the intellect, and that which for want of a better term we may call the wisdom of the spirit." If reality is so structured that man—though fallen from the state of perfect freedom—can grasp himself in a new life of freedom, the possibility of the freedom of proclamation can be understood. Enid Welsford can say of the fool that he "is a creator not of beauty but of spiritual freedom." As reality offers the possibility of spiritual freedom to the fool, it also affords it to the one who seeks to proclaim. The wisdom of the spirit is not bound by "the finality of fact." Another analogy to poetic proclamation can perhaps be found in *play,* of which Johan Huizinga says in *Homo Ludens:* "From the point of view of a world wholly determined by the operation of blind forces, play would be altogether superfluous. Play only becomes possible, thinkable and understandable when an influx of *mind* breaks down the absolute determinism of the cosmos." [54]

(5) Analogies, however, should not make us disregard the specific task of proclamation. In his Wordpresence God shares himself as costly love. In proclamation this sharing becomes concrete. Jesus told the Jews: "I know that you have not the love of God within you." (John 5:42) As man refuses to live by God's love, he rejects God's Wordpresence: "You do not have his word abiding in you." (John 5:38) God sends his Son into the world to make

man aware of the presence of his costly love. Proclamation continues the emphasis. God's costly love is near. Its presence in man's life does not depend on proclamation; but proclamation alerts man to its presence.

(6) Proclamation as the sharing of costly love is diakonic preaching.[55] It is a waiting on man, a diakonic deed. We thus dare not underestimate preaching, as though words were less important than deeds. Preaching is a word-deed. It desires to become incarnate in a total diakonic existence.[56] It presses toward the diakonic deed-word. Preaching takes place in the hope that man in his entire being can be made whole. Man is healed when in word and deed he is grounded again in the primordial Word.

We would be remiss if we failed to state that the primordial Word reaches into the political dimension. Man is only man together with his neighbor. The communal nature of man is threatened most severely today in the realm of politics, local, national and international. Since God in his Wordpresence shares himself with all men, proclamation cannot but seek to draw out the creative possibilities this presence affords for man's social relationships. God as costly love is unceasingly involved in creating opportunities for the fulfilment of man's manhood. Reconciliation is never a principal impossibility for God. Proclamation seeking the creative word that opens for man his true potential will be utterly irrelevant if it leaves out the political dimension. Proclamation can be poetic, that is, truly creative only as political proclamation.

⁌ V ⁍

HERMENEUTIC AND ETHIC

There is such a thing as being too detached.[1]

ALBERT SCHWEITZER

It hardly needs to be stressed that in the present situation of Protestantism the Christian ethic is as much in the melting as the concept of God. John A. T. Robinson writes in this vein: "It is impossible to reassess one's doctrine of God, of how one understands the transcendent, without bringing one's view of morality into the same melting-pot. Indeed, the two are inseparable. For assertions about God are in the last analysis assertions about Love—about the ultimate ground and meaning of personal relationships." [2] The remark reveals the close connection between the hermeneutic of God and the Christian ethic. God gives meaning to man's social existence.

The two concerns, hermeneutic of God and ethic, are not related automatically. The awareness of being that Christian experience seeks to articulate relative to God's costly love is not a postulate of ethical reflection. Man's practical reasoning, the fact that he seeks to come to grips with his responsibility as a social being, is a phenomenon *sui generis*. The etymology of the word "ethic" points to a dimension quite neutral to the quest of God. Paul Lehmann reminds us, humiliating though it may be, "that the term was first applied not to human beings but to animals. It was obvious to men that animals needed to be put somewhere for shelter and protection. Thus the germinal idea in the word τὸ ἦθος is the stability and security provided by a 'stall' or 'dwelling' for animals. The verb root εἴωθα means 'to be accustomed to' or 'to be wont to'. Hence the relationship between stability and custom was a kind of elemental datum of experience. It was really the primary office of custom to do in the human area what the stall did for animals: to provide security and stability." [3] Practical reason seeks to provide some stability for the ordering of life. The most fundamental aspect of forming this stability is the development of habit. Religion in many cultures may provide the basis of the stability. But this is not necessarily so.

It would lead us far afield if we were to examine various ethical systems or postures with respect to their origin in the need for stability in human relations. We are interested in the rationale of the *Christian* ethic, especially the shape of its origin. Why is the Christian ethic tied so closely to the Christian view of God? What specifically in the Christian ethic accounts for the close connection?

THE NEW MORALITY

Today much of the ethical reflection of Protestant theology focuses on what goes by the name "the new morality," a phrase introduced to the Protestant discussion by Bishop Robinson in *Honest to God*. A number of theological factors (and some nontheological ones no less) contributed to its formation. The most recent one was the battle of *neoorthodoxy* versus *liberalism*. Basic to this battle in the field of ethics was the issue whether or not the ethical demands of the New Testament are realizable. The answer of neoorthodoxy was negative. But did the fact that the ethical demands of the New Testament were not realizable mean that they were not valid? Regardless of how much neoorthodox theologians stressed their good intentions, the popular image of their thought contained a measure of doubt as regards validity. It is reflected, for example, in the limerick which appeared after Reinhold Niebuhr had lectured at Swanwick (England):

> "At Swanwick when Niebuhr had quit it
> A young fellow said, 'Now I've hit it—
> Since I cannot do right
> I must find out tonight
> The right sin to commit, and commit it!' " [4]

Although this type of reaction was a misunderstanding, it was widely current. Niebuhr did not want to minimize the validity of the New Testament ethic. But one can easily see how the misunderstanding arose. According to Niebuhr liberalism was deceiving itself by assuming that the ethical demands of the New Testament were realizable in an industrial society. In an early formulation of his position he contended that the moral ideal of love in Jesus' religion is so pure "that the possibility of its realization in history becomes remote." [5] The ethical demands of the New Testament "[cannot] give us specific guidance in the detailed problems of social morality where the relative claims of family, community, class, and nation must be constantly weighed." [6] Realistically speaking, the New Testament ethic presents us anew with "the problem of compromise, the problem of creating and maintaining tentative harmonies of life in the world in terms of the possibilities of the human situation, while yet at the same time preserving the indictment upon all human life of the impossible possibility, the law of love." [7] Niebuhr did not want to deny that love had been embodied by Christians. But he found that it was "impossible to construct a social ethic out of the ideal of love in its pure form." [8] He appealed to "martyrs and saints, missionaries and prophets, apostles and teachers of the faith" who prove that love can be quite real among men. Even so, the average human being caught in the mesh of sinful society had proved incapable of fulfilling the mandate of love. While "the impossibility of an impossible possibility was implicit rather than explicit in the thought of Jesus," prophetic Christianity since St. Paul knows full well of the dialectic between the perfect demand and man's imperfection. The presence of the ideal of love in every moral aspiration and achievement makes man aware of his shortcomings. [9]

This is by no means an adequate restatement of Niebuhr's position, its subtleties and its verve, and especially not of his later work. But it seems a fair summary of the basic stance that lies behind the development of the new morality. Neoorthodoxy wished to establish a rationale for the working of love in justice, so that it could be relevant to life in society. When John A. T. Robinson claims that an *individualistic* love ethic is impossible for the new morality, he appeals to the type of thinking just outlined as the background of the new ethical approach.[10] But while love is as central for Robinson as for Niebuhr, he argues for its relevance in a different way.

Niebuhr was concerned with love *and* justice. But now the stress is more on personal love. As one compares Niebuhr's little volume, *An Interpretation of Christian Ethics*, with Robinson's tract for the times, *Christian Morals Today*, one realizes that ethical reflection has been narrowed down to the mere possibility of *agape*-love. What, if anything, is still valid of the New Testament ethic? The new morality says: *agape*. This needs interpretation—which the new morality is trying to give. And the question that is beginning to loom large is whether the hermeneutic of *agape* is fully understood.

At the core of Bishop Robinson's argument lies the point that *love is above law*. Jesus does not supply the Christian with an ethical code. His purpose was to subject everything in the lives of men "to the overriding, unconditional claim of God's utterly gracious yet utterly demanding rule of righteous love. And men could not acknowledge this claim without accepting the constraint of the same sacrificial, unselfregarding *agape* over all their relations with each other. It is this undeviating claim, this inescapable constraint, which provides the profoundly constant element in the distinctively Christian response in every age or clime." [11] The Christian ethic thus does not consist of invariable propositions. The content of the Christian ethic has changed from generation to generation, not only as regards social, but also with respect to individual or personal ethics. *Agape* as its essence, however, remained the same.

What is the nature of *agape*? Robinson believes that if the Christian "serves people, with no thought for them but as persons, he will discover himself ministering to Christ." So "the presence or absence of love at the deepest level" as concern for persons is the decisive thing in every moral judgment. At this level "persons matter more . . . than any principles." [12] To be concerned for persons does not mean that one wishes to abolish all law. But one wants to see love take precedence: "The deeper one's concern for persons, the more effectively one wants to see love buttressed by law. But if law usurps the place of love because it is safer, that safety is the safety of death." [13]

The authority of the new morality is that of experience. It thinks inductively: "It starts from persons rather than principles, from experienced relationships rather than revealed commandments." [14] The authority here is the empirical and the particular. If this seems to introduce a note of relativity, Robinson is ready to meet the difficulty: "We assume too readily that God is in the rocks but not in the rapids. We identify him instinctively with what is permanent and see ourselves commissioned to stand for the changeless in a welter of chaos not of his making. But that is a Greek assumption, not a Biblical." To make sure that his point is not lost he repeats it once more: "We need not fear flux: God is in the rapids as much as in the rocks, and as Christians we are free to swim and not merely to cling." [15]

There seems no need to stress the importance of the debate about the new morality. Reported *Time* on March 5, 1965: "More than 900 clergymen and students gathered last week at Harvard Divinity School to ponder the new morality and its significance for the church. Inevitably the speakers reached no definitive conclusions, but they generally agreed that in some respects the new morality is a healthy advance, as a genuine effort to take literally St. Paul's teachings that through Christ 'we are delivered from the law.'" At the meeting Joseph Fletcher of the Episcopal Theological School in Cambridge argued that "there is only one thing which is always good regardless of circumstances, and that is neighborly concern, social responsibility, agape—which is a divine imperative." He went on to suggest that in the situational approach of the new morality "one enters into every decision-making moment armed with all the wisdom of the culture, but prepared in one's freedom to suspend and violate any rule, except that one must as responsibly as possible seek the good of one's neighbor." *Time* in its deadpan way concluded: "Which is quite a long thought for an 18-year-old during a passionate moment in the back seat of a car." [16]

As one tries to understand the core of the new morality, one is thrown back upon hermeneutical rudiments. Does this morality unmistakably make it clear that the New Testament is not concerned with an *agape* ethic just for the sake of persons? One does not get the impression that Robinson is saying: What is good for persons is good for ethics. But he does not stress that the good is done in response to God's love, that to be concerned for persons means to obey what truly is.

Neoorthodoxy emphasized that love cannot be realized in society in any simple way. For the new morality love is above the law: we do not need a code; we need concern for persons. The New Testament grounds human love in God's love. Aware of the hermeneutic of God, it points man beyond persons to the source of human personhood. It is impossible for us today to realize the New Testament ethic in detail. But its basic hermeneutical rationale is still valid: we can understand God only as we respond to his love. Apart from this response there is no real point to the Christian ethic.

NONVIOLENCE

God's love is not appropriated in an abstract way. The response to God's love in the New Testament involved a specific action. The recent spread of nonviolence in the United States can serve to clarify the present-day task of Christian ethics as it relates to the New Testament response to God's love.

A dynamic movement for justice confronts us with a model of action repeated over and over again. To some, nonviolence is a means to make the church more relevant. William Robert Miller in his book on nonviolence suggests that nonviolence is "highly compatible with the church and can contribute to its renewal, making it more truly itself." [17] But this can easily be misunderstood unless it is sufficiently interpreted. Nonviolence can only indirectly contribute to the renewal of the church. Miller believes that nonviolence can bear witness to the power of love: "The aim is not merely to be a human punching bag but a witness testifying to the power of love by deeds of truth." The specifically significant aspect of nonviolence is that it involves a model of action: "The core of nonviolence is embedded . . . in the non-violent person's capacity to absorb violence without retaliating." The sit-in is the most well-known form of nonviolent action in which the resister "takes the offensive and moves into the problem area rather than withdrawing from it. It means inaugurating de facto change rather than creating pressure to induce change." [18]

Although the aim of the nonviolent resister is to bear witness to love, Miller knows that nonviolence as such is not a direct expression of love: "It would be specious to argue that a tactic which is intrinsically coercive becomes uncoercive when those who use it profess to be nonviolent. . . . But the Christian realist may find in it a sub-Christian means that is relatively more acceptable than violence or force—a means, moreover, which more readily allows for redemptive modifications." [19] To what, then, does nonviolence give expression? Even Miller wonders whether it might be harnessed "to ends that are violent in spirit." There might be people "motivated by hate or ignorance" who "obstruct justice by 'nonviolent' means." [20] We must face the difficulty right here. The question of motive, as Miller himself points out, cannot be evaded. The motive of Christian action is the response to God's love. This is not a matter of perfectionism, but of the reality by which the Christian lives. Is nonviolence an adequate expression of the Christian's response to God's love?

Our responsibility for a just society is obvious. But the just society is not an end in itself. What the Christian wishes to learn is how God's love can become manifest in society. His response to God's love might demand its own model of action. The dilemma between love and nonviolence is real. Miller has understood this quite well. Since nonviolence is not love, it is not "a method for resolving conflict. It is a way of waging social conflict that is compatible with love. It does a minimum of damage and holds the door open to creative, constructive possibilities. But it has no intrinsic power to heal and to build anew. For this it must look beyond nonviolence to active, agapaic love and reconciliation." [21] Is it impossible for the Christian to wage social conflict directly in terms of his response to God's love? Why should it be possible for the Christian to wage social conflict only in terms of a method that is merely *compatible* with love? Direct nonviolent action is a judgment on the church. She has not as yet developed a model action of her own to express her understanding of God.

Robert W. Spike, in his recent book *The Freedom Revolution and the Churches,* writes about the church: "It knows what the Gospel is, intellectually. The church today is better informed about nuances of theology, liturgy, and the rest than any other generation of Christians, but it finds it painful to acknowledge Christlike action in the world." [22] What is Christlike action? Christ acted with reference to God. We cannot assume that everyone knows what is the most difficult thing to know: God as costly love. Christ's embodiment of costly love was grounded in God: "My food is to do the will of him who sent me, and to accomplish his work." (John 4:34) If we expect everyone to know what Christlike action is, we only increase what is already available in abundance: cheap love. Here we cannot escape the hermeneutical question: Which action refers to God? How can we arrive at the model action that refers to God as a response to his love?

DIAKONIA

Christian decision-making today is often represented as altogether too easy a matter. In some cases it would seem as though nothing else were required as basis for action than a general grasp of human love. Of course, all men know something of love. But God's love was fully embodied only in Jesus. How can we recapture the meaning of Jesus' deed in our action?

The Johannine literature presents the climax of theological reflection on love in the primitive church. Especially significant for our emphasis on man's response to God's love is I John 4:7-21, where for the first time God is equated with love. The passage begins: "Beloved, let us love one another; for love is of God, and he who loves is born of God and knows God. He who does not love does not know God; for God is love." (vv. 7-8)

Those to whom these words were addressed were aware of a distinct meaning of the word *agape* as compared with other Greek words for love, *eros,* the love of desire, and *philia,* the love of friendship.[23] Man had learned to know different loves. While *eros* seems to have reflected the desire for an object, *agape* was understood more as an act of free decision and at times even as a love that stooped down.

Man's general awareness of love was transformed in a new event, the cross of Christ: "In this is love, not that we loved God but that he loved us and sent his Son to be the expiation for our sins." (v. 10) Christ's cross became central for the understanding of love in faith: "By this we know love, that he laid down his life for us." (I John 3:16) The unique history of love in Jesus was joined to man's awareness of love. This historico-ontological fusion (a specific history being joined with man's awareness) has to take place time and again if we want to understand God's love.[24]

The present-day relevance of the historico-ontological union of man's natural awareness of love with faith's understanding of love should be fully grasped. Man is addressed as a being that loves: "Beloved, if God so loved us, we also ought to love one another." (I John 4:11) While modern man does not distinguish between various loves exactly the way the Greeks did, he is also torn by a number of loves. Acceptance of God's love is not experienced merely *verbally* by adding a new word to one's vocabulary or by broadening the meaning of the old word, but by the transformation of one's loves. As the word "love" is baptized for Christian use, man's loves die in order to rise as *costly* love. The transformation is part of man's renewal in the totality of his being.

Central to the Johannine passage, however, are two words and not one: love and God. Since there were many gods in the ancient world, the word "God" had, of course, many meanings. In every instance man's God was the center of his trust. But now it was said that God is love. This meant: what ultimately is is love transformed by the cross, the laying down of a life, costly love. Here the historico-ontological hermeneutic again claimed a word of man's language and related it to the history of Jesus of Nazareth. As the word "God" was christened for use in Christian language, the ontological experience underlying the word "God" died and rose to new life. When we affirm that God is love, we refer to love transformed by the cross: what really is is costly love. Costly love claims man's commitment to what really is, or his failure to understand what really is, and transforms it.[25]

The talk about God as love makes no sense, however, unless we see it in the total context in which the Gospels present Jesus. In his concern for the blind, the lame, the lepers, etc. (cf. Matt. 11:5), it became manifest who God is. God is love by becoming personally involved with man. We said before that the word that best describes Jesus' action is *diakonia*. Jesus took the concept of the *diakonos* and claimed of himself: "I am among you as one who serves." (Luke 22:27) I am among you as a deacon. But in applying it to his action, he also gave the word new meaning. His *diakonia* is a *new diakonia*, a concern for the neighbor that shows itself especially in a regard for the marginal figures of life.

With *diakonia* Jesus established a new ethical habit. We must understand the model character of *diakonia* as action to be translated into different circumstances and situations. If one, for example, assumes that training in nonviolence is necessary, the point must be made that training in *diakonia* is equally necessary. William Robert Miller says: "With prolonged training through socio-drama, nonviolent conduct becomes an easy reflex that can place the cadre in command of a volatile situation." [26] We cannot expect that costly love will be an easy reflex. It must be learned.

The readiness for *diakonia* is founded in the relationship of the disciple to his Lord: "If any one wants to be my deacon, he must follow me; and where I am, there shall my deacon be also." (John 12:26. My own phrasing) To be a deacon means to follow Jesus in personal involvement with the neighbor's needs. A deacon is a disciple who shares in the shape of Jesus' life, not by imitating him, but by using all circumstances of life as opportunities for training in *diakonia*.

It would be wrong to assume that in race relations, for example, a crash program for social justice—as pressing as it is—is the church's only alternative to the perpetuation of irrelevant piety. The mind of the church has to be transformed in *diakonia*. On April 10, 1965, *The Saturday Evening Post* carried an article, "Integration Could Destroy Mississippi," by Dr. Clayton Sullivan. A thirty-four-year old Baptist pastor (who studied at Harvard

Divinity School and Union Theological Seminary) in a small county seat in southwestern Mississippi, he believes that integration would wreck the rural areas of the South. He is especially concerned about the behavioral gap between whites and Negroes: "I wonder if it ever has dawned upon critics of the South that one of the reasons Southerners find the idea of integration so abhorrent is because of the rural Negro's physical uncleanliness? Doctors have discussed with me the difficulties they have in dealing with Negroes who come to them for medical help. Dirt and filth, giving off an emetic stench, often is caked on their patients' bodies. There are dentists in my acquaintance who have told me of Negroes with tartar caked so thickly that it is literally impossible to see their teeth." [27] Dr. Sullivan puts forward some solutions, for example, that rural Negroes should leave the South. The South does not have enough jobs to offer. He also suggests cultural and economic rehabilitation. But he makes no mention of what the church might be able to do as church, not to speak of what the church has failed to do. It is at this point that we must appeal to training in *diakonia*.

It apparently never occurred to Dr. Sullivan that, for example, Jesus' washing of the disciples' feet might have some concrete relationship to the dirt and filth caked to the Negroes' bodies. Who owns the shacks they live in? Who hires them for a song? In assuming responsibility for the ostracized the church would be taking the first step in *diakonia*. Denominationally some churches are beginning to move, slowly but with determination. Most local churches, however, are still blind to the issues or purposely ignore them. Of course, for a solution of the social problems sociological and other technical knowledge is required. But this could become part of the training in *diakonia*. Here we could spend our time more fruitfully than on prayer meetings and revivals.

The place of *diakonia* in contemporary society has been carefully stressed by Harvey Cox. The healing of the city calls for political action rather than weekend work camps: "The weekend work camp, one of the main aspects of the church's diakonia in the city, is wrong in nearly every way. In a city, the way a neighborhood is best maintained, especially where the vast majority of people do not own their own homes, has more to do with learning how to apply political pressure on landlords than with learning how to apply putty with a knife." [28] But it is also at this point that one has to do the hard thinking. It does not take costly love to apply political pressure. What it means to apply political pressure in costly love can only be discovered in learning *diakonia*. We can wield political pressure as Christians only if we are willing to become involved with the neighbor—as the subject of God's total concern, a person who needs the Gospel as much as a cup of coffee or higher wages. The Gospel summons us to erect signs of *God's* love among men estranged from each other. Cox says: "God wants man to be interested not in Him but in his fellow man." [29] God wants us indeed to be interested in the neighbor for the neighbor's sake. But he also wants us and the neighbor to be interested in him: "This is the great and first commandment." (Matt. 22:38) Without interest in God we will hardly show the right interest in the neighbor. If our love is not a response to God's love, we might not even see the neighbor.

Today affording the opportunity for a cup of coffee, a higher wage, or a better home may well be the most direct expression of the Gospel. But it can be a true expression of the Gospel only if it is one side of the coin of which the other reads: "Man shall not live by bread alone, but by every word that proceeds from the mouth of God." (Matt. 4:4)

At this point the New Testament compels a hermeneutic of God to part company with some present-day reflection on Christian ethics. The recovery of *diakonia* does not entitle us to subject God to the neighbor. Love is indeed above the law, but God is above man's love. An ethic hermeneutically grounded in the New Testament ethic is oriented toward God. This does not mean that the answers will be more simple. To the contrary, they will be more difficult. Political pressure has its place. But God takes first place. The Christian is constrained to confront men with God as the ground of man's decision. He is more than the context of decision. He is its source.

As we are moving into an era of new community organization, the relevance of our discussion becomes sharply focused. The Christian, working for the economic and political power of the poor, the ignored and forgotten, remembers that all power is only delegated power. To confront men with God is to remind them that they have a charge to keep, their lives, their energies, their possessions. The Christian seeks to help others to help themselves—in true freedom. Alms, benevolence, "charity," Christmas baskets are fossils of the past. But the mere creation of new power centers is not the true hope of the future. New voting power, new political alignments, etc., are significant factors in man's political and economic progress. These factors, however, contribute to a true fulfilment of man's struggle for a meaningful life only if they become centered in a new worship: a new acknowledgment of the source of man's personal and communal existence. In the new communities that are now emerging the forms of the established churches are obsolete. Even so, unless community organization is grounded in a new communal worship it will soon prove a stagnant and ephemeral thing. There is little lasting self-respect and respect for the neighbor unless there is respect for Him to whom we all are accountable. New community organization calls for an all-embracing renewal. This is a tough and taxing job. "Learning how to apply political pressure" is not insignificant in this context. But it can be truly meaningful only if it is integrated in the diakonic work of a comprehensive renewal of our personal and communal existence.

In our overview of the problem of hermeneutic and ethic we have not mentioned sex, the bomb, war and other pressing ethical problems.[30] Our attempt to articulate Christian responsibility in race relations should serve as an illustration of the direction we believe hermeneutical examination of any ethical issue must take.[31]

THE NEW QUEST OF GOD, HERMENEUTIC AND ETHIC

In the new quest of God there is no lack of ethical concern. Bishop Robinson's new morality represents the attempt of only one participant to come to grips with Christian ethics. Hermeneutical reflection as stressed by the new hermeneutic, however, could serve to focus the ethical concern of the new quest of God. The new hermeneutic in turn needs to be focused in a hermeneutic of God, so that the intention of raising the hermeneutical question in theology might be clearly understood. This becomes especially pressing as regards Christian ethics. Numerous questions are conceivable that might guide the ethical inquiry. From the viewpoint of the hermeneutic of God only one makes hermeneutical sense: What must I *do* to know *God?*

The new hermeneutic with its emphasis on proclamation might benefit considerably from the ethical concern of the new quest of God. Inquiry into the biblical text is never directed merely to the word-deed but also to the deed-word. Fuchs says: *"If Jesus made the voice of love count, and thus made God himself count, then he wanted his hearers to do this too."* [32] But this has to be argued through in terms of the urgent social issues of our day. We must learn again to see concretely the actual unity of systematic theology as acknowledged in hermeneutical reflection: the historico-ontological hermeneutic is not only the foundation of dogmatics but also of ethics. Hermeneutic in theology must clearly articulate its import for ethical decision: "There is such a thing as being too detached." [33]

The ethical significance of the interdependence between the new quest of God and the hermeneutical task of theology is underlined in a recent study by Paul Ramsey, *Deeds and Rules in Christian Ethics.* Ramsey immediately points out that *agape* is the central concept in the present debate of Christian ethics about its task: "The fundamental question concerning the Christian life is whether from *agapé* there comes any instruction concerning the moral life, or any formative influence productive of a Christian style of life." Ramsey sees present-day *agape*-ethics divided up into two camps: act-agapism and rule-agapism. He quotes another ethicist, William K. Frankena, to the effect that in act-agapism "we are to tell what we should do in a particular situation simply by getting clear about the facts of that situation and then asking what is the loving or the most loving thing to do in it." The point is that in act-agapism we are never to appeal to rules. By contrast, rule-agapism tries "to determine what we ought to do, not by asking which *act* is the most loving, but by determining which *rules of action* are most love embodying." [34]

I submit that the whole argument is essentially one about the character of God. Ramsey knows this, too, but he does not make it a central emphasis of his study. For example, he charges Paul Lehmann with keeping us in the dark in his ethics when it comes to knowing what God is doing in the world. He contends that we ought to be "told something more about God's characteristic way of dealing with men than that he—habitually and generally!—plays peek-a-boo from behind the trees in the forest along the road of human history." Ramsey quotes Lehmann as saying: "In the light of God's *characteristic* behaviour there is never any one way as against all others for dealing with any human situation." From this statement Ramsey draws what seems to him an inevitable conclusion: "Since God's 'characteristic' behaviour means that He can be, and likely is, behind two or three trees at once, there is never any one way for Christians to do what He is doing." Ramsey, by contrast, wishes to say that "there is a shape to the gospel of God and a shape to His action that enables us to reflect upon it for our knowledge into God and for our knowledge into the shape of Christian moral action." [35]

This is the crucial point. Love as the costly love of the cross is committed love, a love that works in terms of a specific order. The resurrection affirms that costly love prevails—as God's waiting on man. It is characterized by a certain "predictability." It is reliable, reflecting Jesus' action: "The blind receive their sight and the lame walk, lepers are cleansed and the deaf hear, and the dead are raised up, and the poor have good news preached to them." (Matt. 11:5) In the debate between Ramsey and Lehmann some agreement on the shape of God's action might further understanding. Our essay suggests that Jesus' diakonic acts provide us with a central image for understanding this shape.

Paul Lehmann too wishes to speak of "the behavioral dependability or faithfulness of God." [36] Practically, this apparently means for Lehmann that Jesus Christ is the one who reveals the politics of God, that is, what God is doing in the world to make human life more human. At the core of Lehmann's interpretation of Jesus we find the image of the Messiah: "The messianic image . . . is . . . the crucial image which illuminates what God is doing in the world. . . . The politics of God gives to the church's concern with and about dogma a christological focus and to Christian thinking about ethics a christological foundation." [37] In order to interpret the Messianic image Lehmann uses the Reformers' teaching of Christ's threefold office and points especially, as I understand him, to the prophetic office as that aspect of Christ's ministry which shows what God is doing in the world.

The point Lehmann wishes to make is unmistakable: God is a politician. What still needs to be settled in the Ramsey-Lehmann exchange is what type of politician he is. The qualification we wish to introduce is that God is a politician as a *deacon*. He has tied his politics down to a certain type of action. God is always waiting on man.[38] His action is never a selection from a number of possible actions. It is always his self-limitation to the one possible action.

God's *agape* is itself an order. When St. Paul says in Galatians 6:2, "Bear one another's burdens, and so fulfil the law of Christ," he is appealing to the *nomos* that is part of God's very being. It is in this area that we must try to find an answer to James M. Gustafson's question of ethical principle: "Is there one normative starting-point, or base point, for work in Christian ethics around which other discussion ought to cohere?" [39] Focusing on the law of Christ we might be able to arrive at a clearer understanding of Ramsey's basic point that "Act Agapism drives on to Rule Agapism of some sort." We might learn that human rules can be but reflections of God's "rule" in the *nomos* of his *agape*. Ramsey's assertion that in ethics the Christian "starts with people and not rules" in the context of the hermeneutic of God would have to be centered in the affirmation that the Christian starts with God and his order.[40]

If we center in on God's order, we might learn that the Christian ethic is not so much determined by act-agape or rule-agape as by *diakonia*-agape, so that the ethos of God's Servanthood gives direction to Christian faith and action. The "beyond" of the debate of contextual ethic versus rule ethic lies in God's *diakonia*.

Lehmann's contextual ethic has already taken an important step toward transcending the deadlock of the debate. Lehmann claims: "Christian ethics in the tradition of the Reformation seeks to provide an analysis of the environment of decision in which the principal foundations and preceptual directives of behavior are displaced by *contextual foundations* and *parabolic directives.*" [41] Why could we not draw out more fully the hermeneutical implications of God's *diakonia* as a parabolic directive? Jesus' life as a whole is a parabolic directive—not merely the prophetic office or his office as a king. Jesus' life is a parabolic directive in the sense that he is an embodiment of God's rule. His life is a parable of *God's order.* He does not give us neat rules by which to live. But in understanding his life as a parabolic directive we are driven to embody God's order in a completely new way for our day. We are thus motivated not by laws, but by the spirit of God's *diakonia.*[42]

The hermeneutic of God acknowledges the question of God as primary for Christian ethics. The parabolic directive that is rooted in God's *diakonia* becomes central. This means that the basic biblical thought forms in which God has been acknowledged must be keenly apprehended today as the formative influence of ethical decision. James M. Gustafson, in a survey essay entitled "Christian Ethics," after noting that Americans have done little work in the history of Christian ethics, observes that "they have done less on the relation of ethical thought to biblical scholarship." [43] The work of Harvey Cox, to which we have referred before, is representative of recent efforts among younger Protestant theologians who try to think through the task of Christian ethics with reference to the results of biblical scholarship. But from Cox we can also learn that we are still in the beginnings of arriving at a clear hermeneutical methodology for ethics. For example, Cox uses a thought of Archie Hargraves, who "compares the work of God in the world, where Jesus Christ is present, to a 'floating crap game' and the church to a confirmed gambler whose 'major compulsion upon arising each day is to know where the action is' so he can run and 'dig it.' " [44] Cox apparently approves of the idea. I find it extremely difficult, however, to view the church in this image. One might rather think of the general practitioner, the physician who personally cares for the sick, whose life is committed to be where the sickness is and to heal it. This image at least is not foreign to the parabolic directive centered in Christ: "Those who are well have no need of a physician, but those who are sick; I have not come to call the righteous, but sinners to repentance."

(Luke 5:31–32) The image of the physician corresponds to God's *diakonia*; the image of the gambler does not.

I realize that Cox does not wish to view the entirety of the Christian life in terms of the gambler image. Finding the action is the first step. Shaping the church is the second: "Theology, in these terms, is concerned *first* of all with finding out where the action is. . . . Only then can it begin the work of shaping a church which can get to the action." [45] But it is not easy to discover in Cox in this context the transition from the gambler to the responsible community. "Knocking on doors and urging people to participate in a school stayout" [46] is admirable, but does not necessarily create responsible community. After the "flash in the pan" the situation is usually very much the same as before—as far as the church is concerned. No new community of faith has arisen.

Cox writes: "Metropolitan problems must be dealt with on a metropolitan level, not simply in the inner-city itself. They must be dealt with politically, not only privately. Most important, they must be tackled by groups of people from all sectors of the city who recognize each other as co-responsible for finding solutions. . . ." [47] It is not difficult to find oneself in accord with these suggestions in principle. But people must be *trained* for recognizing each other as co-responsible for finding solutions. There have to be experts who know how changing "bank practices, zoning laws, school financing, and tax structures" can be achieved efficiently. Just as the physician needs training in his craft, the minister needs to engage in a thorough training to be able to lead a group of people toward shaping the church in a new way. Or—if this seems to put an undue stress on the minister—it will take much self-education among the people to be able to shape the church anew while changing bank practices, zoning laws, school financing, and tax structures.

A real threat to meaningful Christian witness in this context is the *ad hoc* congregation. Cox observes: "Ad hoc congregations represent the ecclesiastical equivalent of contextual ethics." [48] Quite so. The *ecclesiastical* equivalent! As such, the *ad hoc* congregation stands as much in need of nonecclesiastical interpretation as the established church. There can be little *ad hoc* about negotiating with welfare departments and City Hall, if one wants to make a dent on a community in the long run. It takes know-how, footwork and a long breath, that is, living with a situation in persistent effort.[49] Here we need trained individuals who are able to make cool political decisions without immediately hankering for *ad hoc* congregations. Without being *persistently* co-responsible for a community, any effort of an individual or a group to change things will hardly be an effort in *diakonia*. Anything *ad hoc* will have great difficulty in reflecting the *law* of Christ, the *order* of God's *diakonia*.[50]

Today we are only in the beginnings. A large share of the responsibility for tackling the task rests with the divinity schools. Little would be gained by adding new courses or new departments. Too much of this has been done already, the proliferation of offerings contributing little to understanding. What is necessary is a reorientation of theological instruction. This is especially true of systematic theology. It must be oriented in social change and develop a program that ties in with courses in politics, sociology, economics, and so forth, in the other departments of the university. Perhaps it would be possible to require one theological course less for graduation and to replace it with a course in the areas just mentioned. Obviously this course would have to be carefully coordinated with the program in systematic theology as a whole. "Clinics" in social change would have to be established, in which the student could become directly involved in relating his theoretical reflection in systematic theology to concrete findings in society.

Work on the Th.M. level offers an especially felicitous opportunity to reorient instruction in systematic theology. Here the student is less restricted to required theology courses. The greater over-all flexibility makes it easier to substitute a course in politics, for example, for a theological course. In the new era into which we have entered, systematic theology will have to sacrifice the abstract examination of some of its language for getting down to the business of life. Only in relationship to concrete life situations can the language of systematic theology become meaningful. The only addition to the program of systematic theology that I can conceive of is a course for laymen that would be part of a total program of instruction for the laity in the skills required today in working with and perhaps solving our political, social, and economic dilemmas.

The responsibility of the church as a whole for developing lay training institutes is a matter I need not try to detail within the confines of this book. A good rule to remember for the reorientation of systematic theology in all instances is *non multa, sed multum*. Not quantity, but quality! [51]

If we seriously consider the implications of God's *diakonia* for the Christian ethic, the issues today boil down to the necessity of acquiring proper skills for handling society's complex problems. The major ethical issue in the church today is ignorance. The debate about the old and the new morality, the concern for love above law, or the challenge to act politically rather than privately can make sense only to the extent that all this contributes to developing the proper skills for handling concrete situations. [52]

The acquiring of skills in the church needs a focus. In its root the ignorance of the church relates to the God-man dimension. Only in the structure of God's *diakonia* does the Christian find the proper rationale for applying his skills to society. Conforming to this structure the Christian ethic can become a *diakonia* ethic.

THE PRESENT-DAY TASK
OF SYSTEMATIC THEOLOGY

*We are clumsy beginners in this language school. But
we know the promise that a saving and healing Word is at
hand even amid the language difficulties of today. That is
why we are theologians and think humbly enough of ourselves but very highly of our task.*[1]

GERHARD EBELING

SYSTEMATIC theology is the critical restatement of the Gospel for
today with reference to the interpretation of the Gospel in the
history of dogma. It is bi-polar. As a restatement of the Gospel it
is concerned with the New Testament texts reflecting the Gospel,
just as much as is exegesis.[2] But it has to consider in equal measure
the contemporary factor. Here the problem of translation is introduced. The texts reflecting the Gospel are language composites.
An analysis of the texts imposes upon us a systematic principle:
the historico-ontological hermeneutic. The language of the Old
Testament and the language of the Graeco-Roman world, as they
became the language of the Christian faith, were christened in the
union of man's understanding of reality (or lack of understanding)
with the witness to Jesus' history. It is this principle that informs
the restatement of the Gospel for today. Its application is what
primarily makes systematic theology systematic. In outlining the
principle we have limited ourselves to the Fourth Gospel, mainly
because it is that book of the New Testament which is most explicit in its hermeneutic.

Another self-limitation must be mentioned. We have tried to

confine ourselves to the basic components of theological understanding. As long as "the nuclear structure" of the theological hermeneutic has not been clearly analyzed, there is little point in examining the more traditional tasks of systematic theology, its accountability to Christian doctrine, etc. Our main concern was the
examination of the word "God" in the context of an analysis of
the elementary hermeneutical components of theology.

Why the word "God" becomes especially important for systematic theology has been briefly stated by Ebeling: "The nature
of systematic theology can be defined only in the context of *the*
word-event which in the name of Jesus brings God, and for that
very reason also the world, to understanding by vindicating
faith." [3] The word-event in the name of Jesus brings God . . . to
understanding! Why God? Systematic theology approaches the
biblical texts with a question. It wants to know in what sense the
Bible speaks of God, especially the New Testament. If systematic
theology does not work under the guidance of this question, it will
soon learn that it has surrendered its task.

The question of God is always raised in a specific context.
Systematic theology analyzes the question as stated by the church.[4]
This we tried to do in our first chapter. We examined the positions of present-day theologians who are wrestling with the question of God. We assumed that they reflect the questing of at least
a significant segment of Protestantism. Someone might suggest
that working under the guidance of the question of God, systematic theology already shows its accountability to Christian doctrine. The point we would wish to make in reply is that the question of God does not as yet reflect any particular doctrine, but
merely the desire to understand the traditional key word of the
Christian language.

The way the word "God" still functions in some Christian
language is that this language says "God *is*." Is there a problem
hidden in the use of the word "is" in connection with the word
"God"? As long as the church affirms that God *is*, systematic theology is obliged to examine the affirmation in the light of the
biblical texts and man's awareness of being.

For the purpose of our conclusion we restate the church's
affirmation that God *is* with reference to John Macquarrie's essay

"How Is Theology Possible?", published in *The Honest to God Debate*. Macquarrie believes that the religious, existentially structured question needs to be formulated in some such way as: " 'Can we regard Being as gracious?' It is a question about the character of grace, so that human life can be lived in the strength of a power from beyond man himself, and ceases to be the tragic contradiction it would be in the absence of grace." He goes on to state that " 'God' is the religious word for Being, understood as gracious. . . . 'Being' can be equated with 'God' only if Being has the character of grace and is responsive to man's existential predicament." [5] In the first chapter I suggested that we must argue the case somewhat differently. The encounter with being raises the problem of articulation. Does being mean anything? Which word can we give it? Is there a primal word for the primal experience? Contemporary man is not sure. Thus we spoke of the ontological aporia.

With the aporia in mind we turned to Jesus' history. Historical reflection as such, however, does not answer man's ontological aporia. The New Testament witness to Jesus' history seems to face the very same difficulty. But in the witness we also discover a creative word that overcomes man's puzzlement: God is love, costly love. This love gives meaning to being and to the religious word for being, the word "God." The historico-ontological hermeneutic affirms: What truly is is costly love.[6]

It may be said that the argument has been drawn up wrong to begin with. The question might be influenced too much by ontological concerns. Harvey Cox claims: "In the age of the secular city, the questions with which we concern ourselves tend to be mostly functional and operational. . . . Secular man relies on himself and his colleagues for answers. He does not ask the church, the priest, or God. . . . So it is pointless and unfair to try to force secular man into asking religious questions, consciously or otherwise, before we can converse." [7] Of course, we should not try to make modern man ask questions he does not raise in the first place. But can secular man escape the search for meaning? He is. He must *be*. Secular man is just as puzzled by what it means to *be* as "ontological" or "mythological" man. Pragmatic as he is, he does not seek his answer in the supernatural or metaphysical. He seeks meaning in belonging or status. Secular man deifies the peer group or his position in the peer group. He too wants to *be*.

Here, rather than in any experience of the transcendent, lies a pre-awareness of what the Gospel affirms, though man might show a complete lack of understanding at this point. Cox believes "that van Buren is wrong when he states that modern, secular man does not experience the transcendent." Modern man might meet the transcendent "as Bonhoeffer once said, 'in the nearest Thou at hand,' but he does meet it." [8] Even if modern man should experience the transcendent, we have to make the hermeneutical implication explicit. What is it that man must come to grips with in his encounter with the nearest "Thou" at hand? What is the experience of the transcendent all about? It is a matter of what it means to be. Especially as regards man's encounter with the nearest "Thou" at hand, the Gospel comes with the claim: What really is is costly love.

In fulfilling its task of restating the Gospel for today, systematic theology stands in a community of scholars who approach the biblical texts historico-critically. This community determines the critical quality of systematic theology. It is especially the method of historical criticism that reveals the historical aporia in the church's attempt to understand the basic datum of faith. Systematic theology realizes that the historico-critical method and the question of God meet in the aporiae. Where history knows of no answer, the question of God still seeks for an answer. In the face of the historical aporia the historico-ontological hermeneutic of the New Testament asserts itself.

The basic hermeneutical principle reveals itself also to the exegete. But the exegete does not try to state the Gospel for today in terms of the shape of this principle under the guidance of the question of God. Exegesis only uncovers the working of the hermeneutical principle in the biblical texts. There is a distinct difference between exegesis as understanding the text and systematic theology as understanding by means of the text. We thus cannot say together with Ebeling that systematic theology, "rightly understood, is an element in all theological disciplines." [9] Exegesis is not partly systematic theology. The same must be said about church history. Exegesis and church history pursue their own interests.

Systematic theology translates the Gospel for today on the model of the historico-ontological hermeneutic in dialogue with previous translations of the Gospel. It was especially in dogma that the historico-ontological hermeneutic found condensed expression. For example, the dogma of the two natures of Christ is a symbolic articulation of the relationship between the ontological and the historical aporiae as transformed by the Christ event.

In addressing itself to its task systematic theology from the very beginning dare not forget, however, that its primary interest is not the dogmatic system: "Rather it is a question of grasping the coherence of the subject in two respects: on the one hand the coherence between faith and reality in the whole range of experience and in all the manifold ways of perceiving truth, on the other hand the coherence between the individual statements of faith as mere modifications of one single statement." [10] While both tasks certainly lie at the center of systematic theology, nothing is gained if the single statement of faith of which all other statements are modifications (in our case the single statement is understood to be the Gospel) is not the nucleus of systematic theology *in terms of its basic hermeneutical structure:* its historico-ontological shape under the guidance of the question of God.

We can perhaps clarify the significance of the discussion about the task of systematic theology with reference to an article by Thomas J. J. Altizer on "Creative Negation in Theology." [11] It is a brilliant exposition of the systematic implications of the so-called death of God theology. Altizer lets us know what to expect of the death of God theology for the future of systematic theology.

Like many others today Altizer believes that theology is losing its bearings: "Only recently the theologian could speak in a pseudo-existential language of crisis and renewal. Yet now we know that the very form and discipline of theology is disappearing beyond the horizon of our historical past." Perhaps in trying to sustain the community of faith it is still possible to appeal to some norm or common ground of theological work. But as regards the witness to the world, one is cut loose from all the traditional moorings: "In this situation theology can continue to maintain its traditional form only by becoming the depository of a Word that has no relevance and therefore no meaning in our world. While such a function may well be essential for the preservation of the community of faith, it must be complemented and challenged by a form of theology that dares to encounter the new world that is dawning in our era, even if such a confrontation condemns theology to a negation of itself." It might be appropriate at this point to indicate that from our point of view theology cannot that neatly divide between a responsibility for the church and a responsibility for the world. The essential questions of both concerns are very much the same.

The basic issue for Altizer is how theology can "preserve a Christian form . . . by speaking an incarnate Word that fully confronts the concrete time and space before it." Theology is supposed to speak "the Christian Word" or "the Word of faith." But how does one get a hold of such a Word? While it may well be the case that to many present-day Christians "the biblical and traditional images of Christ are no longer meaningful," [12] it is impossible to speak of an incarnate Word, a Christian Word or a Word of faith unless one recalls that we could not speak of this Word if there had not been a primal witness to the Word.[13] In fact, it is exactly the biblical word that informs Altizer with the concept of the Christian Word or the Word of faith. Of course, we must speak to the present moment. But we are also involved in a hermeneutical effort when we speak the Christian Word today.[14] We cannot escape translating from the Bible, and translating here is meant in the broadest sense. There is no Christian Word today apart from the texts that reflect the Gospel. And in these texts there is no Christian Word without God. Realizing our dependence on the texts that reflect the Gospel in the New Testament, we cannot help noticing the model of theological thought. We are not at liberty to choose what we like once we commit ourselves to speaking of the Christian Word.

The New Testament does not share itself as a word which is historically confined to a particular time and place. It implies its being grounded in a primordial and eternal Word. Jesus says of his words: "The words I have spoken to you are spirit and life."

(John 6:63) Because these words are grounded in a Wordpresence, they can continue to witness to this Wordpresence as spirit and life. Since these words are tied to the Logos, they can never be merely past. Their meaning may well be hidden to the contemporary mind; therefore we must work out our hermeneutic in order to be able to translate them. In the diakonic word and the diakonic deed Jesus' words take on new meaning today. Without reference to *God* in Christ *in his Word,* however, they remain meaningless.

Altizer claims: "We Christians are called upon to be loyal only to Christ, only to the Incarnate Word who has appeared in our flesh, and therefore we should already have been prepared for the appearance of Christ without God." [15] The difficulty is that *hermeneutically* there can be no Christ *without* God or an Incarnate Word *without* God. In the New Testament Christ does no more than to point beyond himself to God: "He who believes in me, believes not in me but in him who sent me. And he who sees me sees him who sent me." (John 12:44–45) It is inconceivable for the New Testament to believe in an incarnation without God or in a Word of faith without God. If there is a Word *of faith,* does this not mean that there is someone in whom faith is to believe? Otherwise, why faith at all?

I find it difficult to understand why Altizer in this article does not introduce concepts he has used previously. Earlier he could still speak of "the God of the Gospel" or "the God proclaimed by Jesus Christ." At that time he was still looking forward to the recovery in theology of "an eschatological vision of God." [16] Why do these ideas or concepts no longer appear? We are kept guessing, since hermeneutically Altizer is inarticulate. What is his hermeneutical rationale for using some primal Christian categories and neglecting or discarding others? While all of us have preferences and choose some primal categories over others, we have to state our reasons. Is there any primal Christian category that would permit us to drop the word "God"?

It is impossible to proceed theologically at this point unless the hermeneutical commitments are fully made explicit. The hermeneutical grasp of the biblical texts that reflect the Gospel might restrain us from seeking to promote a Christian Word without a primordial Word or a Word without God.[17] As long as the death of God theologians fail to work out their hermeneutic, the reasons for their partial appeal to the biblical word will remain opaque, and conversation will be difficult.[18]

In the confused situation of present-day theology, systematic theology must seek to recover the basic structure of the Christian Word. What lies at the nucleus of Christian language? In its procedure systematic theology is tied to the very language it investigates. Its method is determined by this language—as we have tried to show. There is a model of systematic theology built into the Christian language that we can disregard only at our own peril.[19]

Once one has understood the inevitability of hermeneutic in theology, one still has to state the specific quality of the hermeneutic. We have tried to do this by developing the concept of a historico-ontological hermeneutic. The specific character of this hermeneutic can be lifted out once more in contrast to an essay by Carl Michalson on "The Task of Systematic Theology Today." [20] It is by far the best that has been written on the subject in the sixties thus far and will remain a key essay for years to come. Michalson makes the point that systematic theology cannot operate without a hermeneutic. Our study has not been concerned with what Michalson calls the totalizing hermeneutical process of systematic theology. We were interested only in discovering the method of elementary theological understanding. It has been our contention that the primary present-day task of systematic theology is to focus on this issue. It is the distinct advantage of Michalson's essay that it begins with the problem of the principle of elementary theological understanding, although he does not make this principle focal.

Michalson understands his approach as a whole as a hermeneutic, a hermeneutic of history. He regards Scripture as the formative source of systematic theology and wonders whether the text of theology includes "concerns which resist compression into the single category" of history. Here our accountability to the texts that reflect the Gospel becomes crucial. On what grounds is one entitled to say that "New Testament *theo*-logy may not be a doctrine of God at all but a doctrine of salvation"? [21] It could be that the hermeneutic of history restrains God's freedom to be God. History may be too narrow a category to do justice to the hermeneutic of the New Testament. And it may be that hermeneutic as Michalson defines it is too broad a category to do justice to New Testament history.

The issue here does not relate to some abstract argument, but to the question of the character of the Christian Word. Is our life informed by a lasting reality of truth which claims our response? Or is God's being subject to the changing stream of history as it rolls on with ever increasing momentum?

Among the older generation there is hardly one who has followed the development of what we have called the new quest of God with greater interest than Rudolf Bultmann. It is documented in a 1963 essay, "The Idea of God and Modern Man." [22] After a brief review of some aspects of the quest he states his own position, which is close to that of Michalson. God's being must be understood as historical being, Bultmann says. Thus he appropriates the phrase, coined by Ernst Barlach, of the *metamorphoses of God* (Wandlungen Gottes). The paradox of God's presence in the here and now is always expressed in new forms. Modern man can only accept an idea of God which finds "the Unconditioned in the conditioned . . . and the transcendent in what is present as possibility of encounter." Therefore it is our task "to keep ourselves open for *encounter with God in the world, in time.* Real faith in God is not acknowledgment of an image of God, however correct it might be. Rather it is readiness to encounter the eternal in the present, in the changing situations of our life."

What we wish to stress over against Bultmann—and also Michalson—is that God has not completely "historicized" himself. Although he subjects himself to whatever metamorphoses history suffers, he does not become their slave. Bultmann, if I understand him rightly, also wants to speak of the "unlimited love" of God. In order to be able to speak of God's love, however, as a constant that prevails throughout all historical metamorphoses, Christian language cannot avoid ontological terms. Christian language must speak of God's being, a being not absorbed by history. It cannot do this if God's being becomes subservient to the historical.

This is not theological caprice. Christian language is compelled to speak of God's being as love because of its hermeneutical commitment. Encounter with God is primarily encounter with his Word. It is encounter with God in the metamorphoses of history *only* under the aegis of the encounter with his Word. His transcendence in any encounter is his transcendence in his Word. It is grounded in his Wordpresence. Systematic theology has the task of articulating the hermeneutical effort necessary to understand this unique transcendence.[23]

The most important recent contribution that addresses itself to the problem of God's unique transcendence is Wolf-Dieter Marsch's *Gegenwart Christi in der Gesellschaft*, published in 1965.[24] It is principally a study of the relevance of the early Hegel for present-day theology. Marsch tries to retain the formulation of the theological problem in the early Hegel without becoming captive to the rigid logic of Hegel's later system. His basic presupposition as regards the contemporary theological situation is his rejection of the chasm between the totally transcendent God and man which dialectical theology stresses.

Hegel—in Marsch's view—did not approach the question of God in terms of the alternatives of immanence and transcendence, or time and eternity, but in terms of absolute truth in a context of meaning. Transcendence refers to truth as experienced in history. Hegel sensed the relationship between emancipated control of the world, on the one hand, and loss of a context of total meaning, on the other—the technical shaping of the world *and* the sense of the death of God. At the same time he saw the task of human consciousness not in acquiescing to the loss, but in discovering reconciling centers where life could be reunited.

For Hegel Jesus' life and suffering afforded such a center. In Jesus' sacrifice on the cross absolute love becomes concrete in its self-emptying character. God prevailed in this process that resulted in the death of death; and Jesus' humanity became an element of the divine life.

Jesus becomes present to man today in a basic movement of the human spirit from alienation to reconciliation. Marsch views the polarity between alienation and reconciliation in terms of cross and resurrection. Standing in the world, man must suffer—an experience analogous to Christ's suffering on the cross—and become a free person—analogous to Christ in the resurrection. Suffering the unfulfilled claim of life, man will take the cross of the present upon himself and follow Christ. In expectation of God, he will try to reconcile the promise of life with its actuality. And herein he will become a witness to the resurrection. He must only remember that the life promised in Jesus' resurrection is still an open matter.

Marsch keenly articulates modern man's difficulty in grasping the reality of God. But does the dialectic between alienation and reconciliation make for an easier understanding of God? Can we ever directly translate the historical Good Friday into a contemporary Good Friday? Does not the historical Good Friday speak of the costly love of the man from Nazareth whereas our contemporary alienation speaks of our lack of love? Must we not learn the difference between Jesus' suffering and our suffering before we can think of their analogy? Did not Jesus suffer because of his obedience whereas we suffer because of our disobedience? Was not Jesus' feeling of being forsaken by God the exact opposite of our certainty of the death of God?

We agree with Marsch that the transcendence of God is a transcendence experienced as truth in history. But it is a transcendence that is first of all experienced in the Word of the cross. God appears in this Word. Only in the appropriation of this Word does the movement from unfaith to faith take place. The movement from alienation to reconciliation in society can perhaps reflect the basic movement of faith, but it cannot become its substitute. Our experience of God is still tied to our experience of the Word.

In the beginning of our study we briefly sketched the development of the Protestant theological debate in the last three decades: from the kerygma to the historical Jesus to the being of God. The development has a strangely trinitarian "beat." Perhaps the debate all along has been a wrestle with Spirit, Son, and Father, only now tied to the groping language-search of our bewildered age. Perhaps we are seeking for a new articulation of the Name we have known all along. The problems of communication we are facing in our quest seem overwhelming. "But we know the promise that a saving and healing Word is at hand even amid the language difficulties of today. That is why we are theologians and think humbly enough of ourselves but very highly of our task." [25]

NOTES

NOTES

The notes, besides giving references for material quoted, intend to aid the reader in the use of the bibliography, introducing him also to titles not dealt with in the body of the book. The multiplicity of the notes partly reflects the pluralism of the present theological situation. Translations, wherever necessary in the text or in the notes, are my own. Biblical quotations, unless otherwise indicated, are from the RSV.

CHAPTER I

1. Saul Bellow, *Herzog* (New York, 1964), p. 340.

2. There is a parallel development in Roman Catholic theology, although with different accents. See, for example, Gustave Weigel, S. J., *The Modern God* (New York and London, 1963), John Courtney Murray, S. J., *The Problem of God* (New Haven and London, 1964), and R. W. Gleason, S. J., *The Search for God* (New York, 1964).

3. The classic account of the development is still James M. Robinson, *A New Quest of the Historical Jesus* (Naperville, 1959).

4. Rudolf Bultmann, "New Testament and Mythology," in Hans Werner Bartsch, ed., *Kerygma and Myth* (New York, 1961), pp. 43f.

5. See the remark with which the editors introduce the essay by Langdon Gilkey, "Secularism's Impact on Contemporary Theology," *Christianity and Crisis*, 25 (April 5, 1965), p. 64. See also the editorial "Comment" in the *Christian Advocate*, 9:19 (October 7, 1965), p. 2.

6. Martin E. Marty and Dean G. Peerman, eds., *New Theology No. 2* (New York and London, 1965), p. 8. Cf. Eberhard Jüngel, *Gottes Sein ist im Werden* (Tübingen, 1965), p. 1: "God's being is discussed. This seems to be one way to describe the passionate debate in which present-day Protestant theology is engaged."

7. Langdon Gilkey, "Dissolution and Reconstruction in Theology," *The Christian Century*, 82:5 (February 3, 1965), pp. 136f.

8. My attention has been called to the lack of precision with which the word "referent" is presently being used in theology. For a definition of "referent," see L. S. Stebbing, *A Modern Introduction to Logic* (New York, 1930), pp. 13 and 111. In Stebbing *that which is signified* is called "referend" rather than referent. The fact that *Webster's Third New International Dic-*

tionary seems to approve the broader use of the term "referent" is no justification of logical imprecision. Our argument, however, does not hinge on the term. Suffice it to indicate at this point the logical inadequacy of the word "referent" when it stands for *that which is signified*.

9. Robert W. Funk, "Colloquium on Hermeneutics," *Theology Today*, 21:3 (October, 1964), p. 304.

10. Ernst Fuchs, *Hermeneutik* (Bad Cannstatt, 1958), p. 110.

11. Gilkey, "Dissolution and Reconstruction in Theology," p. 137.

12. H. P. Rickman in Wilhelm Dilthey, *Pattern and Meaning in History* (New York, 1962), pp. 39f. Cf. Michael Polanyi, *Personal Knowledge* (Chicago, 1958), p. 90: "What I *understand* in this manner has a meaning for me, and it has this meaning in itself, and not as a sign has meaning when denoting an object." It is possible that in our present-day wrestle to delimit an area of understanding distinct from knowledge, we are only repeating the battle of the early Hegel. See Richard Kroner, "Hegel's Philosophical Development," Introduction to Friedrich Hegel, *On Christianity* (New York, 1961), pp. 24ff.

13. Wilhelm Dilthey, p. 77.

14. Gerhard Ebeling, *Word and Faith* (Philadelphia, 1963), p. 318.

15. See James M. Robinson and John B. Cobb, Jr., eds., *The New Hermeneutic* (New York, Evanston, and London, 1964). The concept of hermeneutic attained a significant place in Protestant theology through Friedrich Schleiermacher. See also Richard R. Niebuhr, *Schleiermacher on Christ and Religion* (New York, 1964), pp. 82ff. Since Schleiermacher's day, hermeneutic as the art of understanding has had its ups and downs in Protestant theology. But it has never been completely banished from its premises.

16. Recently there has been some discussion of the difference between hermeneutic and hermeneutics. See Robinson and Cobb, *The New Hermeneutic*, pp. 52ff. The term "hermeneutic" has occasionally been used before in the English for what usually has been called hermeneutics. See, for example, Philip Schaff, *Theological Propaedeutic* (New York, 1912), p. 186. The meaning of the term today still depends very much on its specific definition. We speak of hermeneutic as the *method* of understanding.

17. See James W. Woelfel, " 'Non-Metaphysical' Christian Philosophy and Linguistic Philosophy," in Marty and Peerman, *New Theology No. 2*, p. 53: "The significance of *New Essays* should not be underestimated by thoughtful Christians. It is a monument to the possibility of serious and intelligent discussion between Christian and non-Christian in our day."

18. As to theological method, our position is close to that of Jürgen Moltmann, *Theologie der Hoffnung* (München, 1964), p. 128: We move ". . . from the historically-unique to the universal. . . ."

19. John A. T. Robinson, *Honest to God* (Philadelphia, 1963), p. 17.

20. *Ibid.*, p. 29.   21. *Ibid.*, p. 49.   22. *Ibid.*, p. 128.

23. *Ibid.*, pp. 99ff. Cf. William O. Fennell, "The Theology of True Secularity," in Marty and Peerman, p. 29.

24. For a more elaborate critique of Robinson's position, see C. D. Armstrong, "Christianity without Religion," in Marty and Peerman, pp. 23–27.

25. Robinson, p. 129.

26. On p. 86 of *Honest to God* (footnote no. 2), Robinson tells us how he understands and uses the term "religion."

27. David L. Edwards, ed., *The Honest to God Debate* (Philadelphia, 1963), pp. 232–275.

28. *Ibid.*, pp. 249, 251.   29. *Ibid.*, p. 187.

30. See Robinson, *Honest to God*, pp. 55, 61.

31. *The Honest to God Debate*, p. 24. Cf. Albert H. van den Heuvel, "The Honest to God Debate in Ecumenical Perspective," *The Ecumenical Review*, 16:3 (April, 1964), p. 288: "The fundamental question in the *Honest to God* debate is the question of the laity come of age. If the laymen are to be productive, vocal, meaningful members of the missionary church, they have to become partners of the theologians in the formulation, the sharpening and the answering of the questions which need to be treated theologically. . . . The *Honest to God* debate has shown that we have not yet started that process, and that may be its most important contribution to theology today."

32. *The Honest to God Debate*, p. 214.

33. Robinson, *Honest to God*, p. 47.   34. *Ibid.*, p. 54.

35. Cf. William Hordern, *Speaking of God: The Nature and Purpose of Theological Language* (New York, 1964), p. 114. See also the succinct argument in critical assessment of Bishop Robinson's position in Ian T. Ramsey, *Christian Discourse: Some Logical Explorations* (London, New York, and Toronto, 1965), pp. 73ff.

36. Helmut Gollwitzer, *The Existence of God as Confessed by Faith* (Philadelphia, 1965), pp. 247–253.

37. Thomas J. J. Altizer, "The Death of God: Is This Our Situation?" *Christian Advocate*, 9:19 (October 7, 1965), pp. 9f.

38. For the material upon which the following review of Gollwitzer's position is based, see *The Existence of God as Confessed by Faith*, pp. 78, 84, 117, 130, 133, 140, 161, 185, 199.

39. *Ibid.*, p. 212. Cf. the critique of Gollwitzer's view of the word "is" as used for God in Eberhard Jüngel, *Gottes Sein ist im Werden* (Tübingen, 1965), pp. 2–8.

40. For the material reviewed in this paragraph, see Gollwitzer, pp. 121, 135, 141, 152, 182, 213, 222.

41. *The Honest to God Debate*, p. 250.

42. Paul M. van Buren, *The Secular Meaning of the Gospel* (New York and London, 1963), pp. 199f.

43. *Ibid.*, pp. 100f.   44. *Ibid.*, p. 102.   45. *Ibid.*, p. 106.

46. *Ibid.*, p. 139.   47. *Ibid.*, p. 141.   48. *Ibid.*, p. 200.

49. As regards my principal appreciation of van Buren's book, I find that I agree with John Macquarrie, "How Can We Think of God?" *Theology Today*, 22:2 (July, 1965), p. 198: "I have so much admiration for the honesty and courage of this book in facing the predicament of faith today that I regret very much to speak critically of it. But it seems to me that van Buren's attempt to assimilate all theology to christology suffers from the same errors as had already appeared in Herrmann."

50. The basic objection to van Buren's method of the "blik" has been quite sufficiently stated by Van A. Harvey, "The Nature and Function of Faith," *The Christian Century*, 82:31 (August 4, 1965), p. 964.

51. For an over-all critique of van Buren's argument, see Langdon B. Gilkey, "A New Linguistic Madness," in Marty and Peerman, pp. 39–49.

52. Cf. the comment of Langdon Gilkey, "Dissolution and Reconstruction in Theology," p. 137, as regards the secular interpretation of life in general. Gilkey feels "that a 'secular' account of man's existence is too thin, too lacking in the dimension of depth and of mystery, of ultimate joy and of ultimate terror, to reveal the wonder and meaning of life, or of its demonic depths and ever threatening nothingness."

53. William Hamilton, "The Death of God Theology," *The Christian Scholar*, 48:1 (Spring, 1965), pp. 27–48. The following quotes are drawn from this article. For a well-balanced assessment of "The Death of God Theology," see Gabriel J. Fackre, "The Death and Life of God," *Theology and Life*, 8:3 (Fall, 1965), pp. 185–191. The response to this "new" theology at the grass roots has been mixed. A widely prevalent reaction is reflected in the comment of Duncan Norton-Taylor: "There is a current wavelet generated by a handful of young theologians who are putting forward the old Nietzschean dogma that 'God is dead.' It's hard to see how they can be taken seriously, although they are sometimes the center of small storms at seminaries and dinner parties." "What on Earth Is Happening to Protestantism," *Fortune* (December, 1965), p. 173. The best critique of the theological thrust of the movement that has come to my attention thus far has been written by a Jew. See Elmer Berger, "On the 'Death of God' Theologies," *Education in Judaism*, 13:1 (January, 1966), 4 pages. The extent to which the "Death of God Theology" reflects the modern sensi-

bility reminds me of Giorgio de Chirico's *The Return of the Prodigal Son*. In this modern painting God (the Father) has become a lifeless white marble statue and the returning son a faceless robot.

54. The article was "foreshadowed" in chapter 2, "Belief in a Time of the Death of God," of Hamilton's book *The New Essence of Christianity* (New York, 1961), pp. 35–68. For a placing of the death of God theology in the American theological context, see Gene Reeves, "A Look at Contemporary American Theology," *Religion in Life*, 34:4 (Autumn, 1965), pp. 511–525; William Hamilton, "Radicalism and the Death of God," *Christianity and Crisis*, 25:21 (December 13, 1965), pp. 271–273.

55. As to the German debate, see Jürgen Moltmann, *Theologie der Hoffnung*, pp. 150–155. Moltmann here discusses the problem of the "Death of God" from the European perspective. Cf. Gerhard Ebeling, "Existenz zwischen Gott und Gott," *Zeitschrift für Theologie und Kirche*, 62:1 (May, 1965), p. 109. Ebeling here speaks of the "dead, the radically absent, and yet in his absence present God."

56. Gilkey, "Dissolution and Reconstruction in Theology," p. 138.

57. Hamilton, "The Death of God Theology."   58. *Ibid.*

59. John B. Cobb, Jr., *A Christian Natural Theology* (Philadelphia, 1965), p. 14.

60. *Ibid.*, p. 149.   61. *Ibid.*, pp. 170, 173.   62. *Ibid.*, p. 174.

63. It is clear to me that there are other problems connected with the relationship between philosophy and theology for which the examination of Whitehead's philosophy by a theologian might provide a model. Cf., for example, Daniel Day Williams, "How Does God Act?: An Essay in Whitehead's Metaphysics," in William L. Reese and Eugene Freeman, eds., *Process and Divinity: The Hartshorne Festschrift* (LaSalle, 1964), pp. 161–180. Williams' reflections are perhaps best characterized by the following claim: "God makes a specific and observable difference in the behavior of things. . . . Whitehead describes God's actions in such a way that at least some of the traditional difficulties in relating this view to scientific understanding are overcome." (p. 178) Even so, there are very definite limitations for theological assertions: "We have no way of extricating the acts of God from their involvement in the activities of the world." (p. 180) Compare this with Gerhard Ebeling, *Word and Faith*, p. 345: "The reality of God . . . is on no account to be thought of like the reality of the world and consequently as a piece of the world's reality; nevertheless the reality of God can be expressed solely in view of the reality of the world." See also the analysis by Norman Pittenger, "A Contemporary Trend in North American Theology: Process-Thought and Christian Faith," *Religion in Life*, 34:4 (Autumn, 1965), pp. 500–510.

64. Cobb, p. 173.

65. *Ibid.*, p. 253. When I say that I do not object to Cobb's broad definition of theology, I wish to imply that one should not immediately question his intention. It is conceivable that in terms of principle this approach might work out. But then one also has to consider what Cobb actually has done with it. Much of what I object to as regards the actual consequences of Cobb's concept of theology has been articulated in Langdon Gilkey's review of the book, *Theology Today*, 22:4 (January, 1966), pp. 530–545. Gilkey's keen critical tools soon get to the heart of the matter, the quite uncritical acceptance of Whitehead at crucial points: "The rather surprising set of unexperienced things that exist in the Whiteheadian world: prehensions, subjective forms, initial aims, and those omnipresent feelings, are simply assumed without further ado to be *real*, and this complicated picture to be the deepest and most certain sort of truth." So "the method of this philosophical theology seems to be to translate any concept we are seeking to understand or to test into Whiteheadian terms, and to leave the matter at that." According to Gilkey, Whitehead sees "an undistorted and unfallen universe." But, says Gilkey, there are Christian themes "found both in Scripture and in the tradition, which are in marked tension with this vision of an unspoiled if still uncompleted reality." It is impossibe simply to equate the Christian vision of God with the Whiteheadian philosophical vision of God: "Thus a simple God of order, while philosophically coherent, cannot easily be a God of forgiveness as well. . . . It was mainly on this account that Cobb's book seemed to me to break no new ground. Far from challenging or even transforming Whitehead's vision or his categories—as every theologian must do to even the most admired of philosophical masters—he seemed to submit more docilely than the master himself to the rigors of their demands, and even to chastise their originator for occasionally bursting out of their grip."

66. William Hordern, *Speaking of God: The Nature and Purpose of Theological Language* (New York and London, 1964), pp. 113f.

67. *Ibid.*, pp. 119ff.   68. *Ibid.*, p. 116.

69. *Ibid.*, pp. 190f.   70. *Ibid.*, p. 197.   71. *Ibid.*, p. 90.

72. It is difficult to understand why some theologians today wish to create a uniquely American theology. There is as little point in developing an American theology as in trying to develop an Australian physics or an African biology. See Thomas J. J. Altizer, "Amerika und die Zukunft der Theologie," in *Antaios*, 5:5 (January, 1964), pp. 424–436. See also Joseph Haroutunian, "Theology and American Experience," *Dialog*, 4:3 (Summer, 1965), pp. 171–179.

73. Robinson, *Honest to God*, p. 21.

74. Cf. Ian T. Ramsey, *Models and Mystery* (London, New York, and Toronto, 1964), p. 20. Ramsey speaks of ontological commitment: "The ontological commitment arises in a disclosure. . . ." As regards the point-

lessness of reintroducing the religious presupposition, see Arend Th. van Leeuwen, *Christianity in World History* (New York, 1966), pp. 414ff.

75. Gilkey, "Dissolution and Reconstruction in Theology," p. 137.

76. Karl Barth, *Church Dogmatics* (New York, 1957), II:1, p. 260. Cf. Gerhard Ebeling, "Existenz zwischen Gott und Gott," p. 94: "That God is—this is, if one knows what one is saying, the sum of Christian proclamation and Christian faith."

77. Cf. James M. Robinson and John B. Cobb, Jr., eds., *The Later Heidegger and Theology* (New York, Evanston, and London, 1963), pp. 21ff.

78. Schubert M. Ogden, "Theology and Philosophy: A New Phase of the Discussion," *The Journal of Religion*, 44:1 (January, 1964), pp. 11f.

79. Cf. the comment of John Macquarrie in *The Honest to God Debate*, p. 190: "All those who tried to prove the existence of God already believed in him, and must have had a more primordial source for their conviction than their own arguments." Cf. also John Hick, ed., *The Existence of God* (New York and London, 1964), p. 19: "If there is a God, this is a fact which must be known in some other way than by means of philosophical argumentation."

80. Perhaps one understands Schubert M. Ogden's concern for Hartshorne best as an attempt to correct Bultmann's anthropologically-centered theology. Ogden's essay in which he compares Hartshorne and Bultmann is one of the best analyses of the deficiencies of Bultmann's theology from the viewpoint of systematic theology. See "Bultmann's Demythologizing and Hartshorne's Dipolar Theism," in William L. Reese and Eugene Freeman, eds., *Process and Divinity: The Hartshorne Festschrift* (LaSalle, 1964), pp. 493–513. As regards the significance of Hartshorne, note the following statement of Ogden: "The chief distinction of Hartshorne's achievement is that he has succeeded in working out with an unprecedented scope and depth precisely the kind of philosophical theology to which Bultmann's concerns clearly point." (pp. 505f.) See also Schubert M. Ogden, "The Possibility and Task of Philosophical Theology," *Union Seminary Quarterly Review*, 20:3 (March, 1965), pp. 271–279.

81. See Jürgen Moltmann, *Theologie der Hoffnung*, p. 250. Moltmann feels that the proofs for the existence of God have been replaced by hermeneutical reflections.

82. Paul Tillich, *Systematic Theology*, Vol. I (Chicago, 1951), p. 205.

83. *Ibid.*, p. 206.

84. Rudolf Otto, *The Idea of the Holy* (New York, 1958), p. 11.

85. Cf. Ian T. Ramsey, "On Understanding Mystery," *The Chicago Theological Seminary Register*, 53:5 (May, 1963), p. 8: "So we see how we

might continue the tale, develop whatever model we choose for being . . . until we reach the point at which a disclosure is evolved, when everything collapses into immediacy, if I may pilfer a phrase from Hegel."

86. Bellow, *loc. cit.*

87. Bertolt Brecht, *Selected Poems*, trans. by H. R. Hays (New York and London, 1959), p. 63.

88. Cf. Langdon B. Gilkey, "God Is Not Dead," *The Voice*, 57:1 (January, 1965), p. 10: "To analyze these depths, then, is not necessarily to find God; a Void may be found there."

89. Cf. Kornelius Heiko Miskotte, *Wenn die Götter schweigen* (München, 1963), pp. 32 and 64. Miskotte argues quite cogently that religion is not dead in modern man. He makes the equally strong point, however, that the survival of religion does not amount to an appreciable difference for the acceptability of the Christian faith.

90. Martin Heidegger, *Holzwege* (Frankfurt, 1957), p. 186.

91. Tillich, *op. cit.*, p. 238.

92. Wolfhart Pannenberg, *Grundzüge der Christologie* (Gütersloh, 1964), p. 129.

93. Wolfhart Pannenberg, "Die Frage nach Gott," *Evangelische Theologie*, 25:4–5 (April–May, 1965), pp. 238–262.

94. In Robinson and Cobb, *The Later Heidegger and Theology*, p. 35.

95. Hans Jonas, "Heidegger and Theology," *The Review of Metaphysics*, 18:2 (December, 1964), p. 221, indicates that in Heidegger's terms God is a being through which Being reveals itself: "Thus the primal thinking of God is a thinking away from God or a thinking beyond God." Theology in the end is not aided by Heidegger's approach, except in a negative way: we discover the limits of human understanding. Notwithstanding much that has been written in favor of the significance of the later Heidegger for theology in recent years, I believe Erich Dinkler's principal assessment of a decade ago still remains incontrovertible: "It is very hard, indeed, to enter a dialogue with the Heidegger of recent years, since reason and logicism are indispensible for any sort of dialogue and discussion. When thought is interpreted as listening to the dictating Being as such, it becomes inspiration. It is made into an authority, reasonable thinking is dismissed, and a fundamentalistic philosophy is established." Erich Dinkler, "Martin Heidegger," in Carl Michalson, ed., *Christianity and the Existentialists* (New York, 1956), p. 125.

96. Martin Heidegger, *Was ist Metaphysik?* (Frankfurt, 1951), p. 13.

97. Martin Heidegger, *Unterwegs zur Sprache* (Pfullingen, 1959), p. 216.

98. Cf. Hans Jonas, "Heidegger and Theology," p. 219. Jonas claims that Heidegger cannot get beyond the world. Theology should guard the

radical transcendence of God, "whose voice comes not out of being but breaks into the kingdom of being from without."

99. Ebeling, *Word and Faith*, p. 348.

100. Cf. Lawrence A. Larson, "The Pawnbroker," *Christian Advocate*, 9:19 (October 7, 1965), p. 10.

CHAPTER II

1. Dag Hammarskjöld, *Markings* (New York, 1964), p. 68.

2. Albert Schweitzer, *The Quest of the Historical Jesus* (New York, 1948), p. 4.

3. Gerhard Ebeling, *Theologie und Verkündigung* (Tübingen, 1962), pp. 81ff. Cf. Hugh Anderson, *Jesus and Christian Origins* (New York, 1964), p. vii: "Jesus of Nazareth has in fact become *our* biggest problem."

4. The understanding that we study any subject, texts, monuments, etc., with a particular question in mind is nothing new. But only now are we beginning to see it functioning in theology in various contexts of theological concern. See Rudolf Bultmann, "Das Problem der Hermeneutik," in *Glauben und Verstehen*, Vol. II (Tübingen, 1952), pp. 227ff.

5. James M. Robinson, *A New Quest of the Historical Jesus* (Naperville, 1959), p. 75.

6. Rudolf Bultmann and Karl Kundsin, *Form Criticism* (New York, 1962), p. 60.

7. *Ibid.*, p. 68.   8. *Ibid.*, p. 70.

9. William Wrede, *Das Messiasgeheimnis in den Evangelien* (Göttingen, 1901), pp. 129ff.

10. *Ibid.*, pp. 22f.

11. Birger Gerhardsson, *Memory and Manuscript* (Uppsala, 1961), p. 13. For a critical evaluation of the Gerhardsson thesis, see Harvey K. McArthur, "A Survey of Recent Gospel Research," in Martin E. Marty and Dean G. Peerman, eds., *New Theology No. 2* (New York and London, 1965), pp. 201–221.

12. Gerhardsson, pp. 295ff.   13. *Ibid.*, pp. 328f.

14. *Ibid.*, p. 230.   15. Schweitzer, *op. cit.*, p 330.

16. *Ibid.*, pp. 350f.   17. *Ibid.*, p. 387.

18. Cf. Albert Schweitzer, *Paul and His Interpreters* (London, 1948), p. 238.

19. Martin Werner, *The Formation of Christian Dogma* (New York, 1957), pp. 22f.

20. Felix Flückiger, *Der Ursprung des christlichen Dogmas* (Zollikon-Zürich, 1955), pp. 11ff.

21. *Ibid.*, pp. 131f.   22. *Ibid.*, p. 209.

23. See *A New Quest of the Historical Jesus*, p. 31: " 'The historical Jesus' comes really to mean no more than 'the historian's Jesus'. The clear implication is that 'Jesus of Nazareth as he actually was' may be considerably more than or quite different from 'the historical Jesus'."

24. *Ibid.*, p. 44.   25. *Ibid.*, p. 42.

26. *Ibid.*, pp. 71f. As regards the new understanding of history, Robinson appeals to Heidegger and Collingwood.

27. *Ibid.*, pp. 79f.   28. *Ibid.*, p. 92.

29. Hugh Anderson, *Jesus and Christian Origins*, p. 314.

30. For the quote see David L. Edwards, ed., *The Honest to God Debate* (Philadelphia, 1963), p. 252.

31. Martin E. Marty in *The Christian Century* (June 24, 1964), p. 832.

32. Gerhard Ebeling, *Word and Faith* (Philadelphia, 1963), pp. 288–304.

33. *Ibid.*, p. 372.   34. See *ibid.*, p. 302.

35. Carl Michalson, *The Rationality of Faith* (New York, 1963), pp. 18f.

36. *Ibid.*, pp. 98, 105.   37. *Ibid.*, p. 52.

38. *Ibid.*, p. 146.   39. *Ibid.*, p. 64.

40. Paul M. van Buren, *The Secular Meaning of the Gospel* (New York and London, 1963), p. 145.

41. *Ibid.*, p. 125.

42. I have discussed the issue more extensively in an article on the new quest of the historical Jesus, "Possibilities and Limits of the New Quest," *The Journal of Religion*, 43:3 (July, 1963), pp. 218–233. As regards the problem of the significance of the historico-critical method in present-day Jesus research, cf. P. Joseph Cahill, S. J., "Rudolf Bultmann and Post-Bultmann Tendencies," in Marty and Peerman, pp. 222–254.

43. *A New Quest of the Historical Jesus*, pp. 76–80.

44. Heinrich Ott's view in James M. Robinson and John B. Cobb. Jr., eds., *The Later Heidegger and Theology* (New York, Evanston, and London, 1963), p. 83, that the systematician has some supervision over the work of the exegete needs qualification. There is a point where the work of the systematic theologian overlaps with that of the exegete. The systematic theologian must find out in the biblical texts what the nucleus of theological

hermeneutic is. But this does not as such give him supervision over the work of the exegete.

45. Paul Tillich, *Systematic Theology*, Vol. I (Chicago, 1951), p. 133.

46. Ernst Fuchs, *Hermeneutik* (Bad Cannstatt, 1958), p. 157.

47. While Ian T. Ramsey in "On Being Articulate about the Gospel," *The Chicago Theological Seminary Register*, 53:5 (May, 1963), p. 15, clearly sees that "it is all too easy to read the Crucifixion narrative as 'mere matter of fact' without disclosure point," he does not make it intelligible for me how "the disclosure of God in Christ" (p. 19) evolved historically. Hermeneutically, I believe, it is necessary to begin with the disclosure of God in Christ in the crucifixion and to move from there to the resurrection, transfiguration, etc.

48. Wolfhart Pannenberg, *Grundzüge der Christologie* (Gütersloh, 1964), p. 107.

49. *Ibid.*, p. 69.

50. For a theological critique of Pannenberg's position, see Jürgen Moltmann, *Theologie der Hoffnung* (München, 1964), pp. 67–74. See also the critical assessment of Pannenberg's method in Carl E. Braaten, "The Current Controversy on Revelation: Pannenberg and His Critics," *The Journal of Religion*, 45:3 (July, 1965), pp. 231ff. Note especially the question of Ernst Fuchs, p. 231: "Why would I need to have faith if so much trust can be placed on our rational knowledge of the historical past?"

51. Hammarskjöld, *loc. cit.*

52. Theologically, of course, more is at stake than a particular view of the resurrection. Basic to the theological debate about history is the relationship between *faith* and history. See Moltmann, p. 136: "Faith liberates from history."

53. Cf. Jürgen Moltmann, p. 224. For Moltmann it is not only necessary to see the limitations of the human spirit in assessing historical phenomena, but also the limitations of history itself which, having not as yet reached its consummation, is fragmentary and dark.

54. *Time* (April 24, 1964), p. 79.

55. It has not been my intention in this chapter to belittle the historico-causal method or any other method that seeks to come to terms with historical phenomena. What I wish to avoid is the "apotheosis" of any one model of history. I also wish to avoid the apotheosis of any one model to interpret life or reality as a whole. The theologian is entitled to look at his subject matter in terms of more than one model like any scholar. Regardless of whether or not Thorleif Boman adequately interprets the respective structures of Hebrew and Greek thought, the conclusion of his *Hebrew Thought Compared with Greek* (Philadelphia, 1960) reflects the proper method of the

scholar and can serve as example of one possibility of theological scholarship: "The Nestor of modern atomic physics, Niels Bohr, has continually empha- sized that the findings of atomic physics are *complementary*, i.e., they cannot be correctly described without resorting to expressions which are logically ir- reconcilable. Thus, some experiments show that the atom has wave structure, and others show that it consists of particles (quanta). If both are right, reality possesses opposite properties which complete each other. Bohr calls the unitariness of opposite manifestations of a phenomenon *complementarity*. In that sense, Hebrew and Greek thinking are complementary; the Greeks describe reality as *being*, the Hebrews as *movement*. Reality is, however, both at the same time; this is logically impossible, and yet it is correct." (pp. 207f.) On grounds of similar methodological reflections I find it impossible, for example, to accept Carl Michalson's view that if "systematic theology does continue to exist as an independent discipline, it should take the shape not of an ontological but of an historical hermeneutic." Carl Michalson, "The- ology as Ontology and as History," in Robinson and Cobb, *The Later Heideg- ger and Theology*, p. 156.

CHAPTER III

1. Vincent van Gogh, *Letters to Emile Bernard* (New York, 1938), pp. 44f. Cf. William Ellery Leonard, *The Poet of Galilee* (New York, 1928), p. 118: "Jesus is perhaps the greatest artist the Jewish race has produced."

2. John A. T. Robinson, *The New Reformation?* (Philadelphia, 1965), p. 35.

3. Paul M. van Buren, *The Secular Meaning of the Gospel* (New York and London, 1963), p. 146.

4. We note, for example, the significance of the Fourth Gospel in Ernst Fuchs, *Hermeneutik: Ergänzungsheft* (Bad Cannstatt, 1958), pp. 7ff.

5. Edwyn C. Hoskyns, *The Fourth Gospel* (London, 1940), p. 67. (The commentary was edited by Francis N. Davey. In order not to complicate matters we shall refer to all ideas as belonging to Hoskyns.) The question of historical fact in the Fourth Gospel is insoluble at the present state of re- search. It is unlikely that the author was an eyewitness. Westcott's classical argument is well-known. Suffice it to repeat the basic thesis: the author was a Jew, a Palestinian Jew, an eyewitness, an apostle, in fact, the apostle John. The most that present research can claim is that "here and there behind the Johannine narrative there lies eye-witness material." C. K. Barrett, *The Gospel According to St John* (London, 1955), p. 104. John A. T. Robinson argues that the question of authorship is not crucial. What we should be concerned about is the status and origin of the Johannine tradition: "Did this come out of the blue round about the year A.D. 100? Or is there a real continuity, not merely in the memory of one old man, but in the life of an on-going com-

munity, with the earliest days of Christianity?" Robinson's own answer is affirmative. John A. T. Robinson, "The New Look on the Fourth Gospel," in *Studia Evangelica* (Berlin, 1959), p. 350. Once one has agreed upon the reliability of a separate tradition, the next question to tackle is the relationship between the Johannine tradition and the Synoptics. Oscar Cullmann addresses himself to this problem: "Both forms of Christianity existed from the beginning because both found their roots in forms of Judaism present in Palestine." Oscar Cullmann, "The Significance of the Qumran Texts for Research into the Beginnings of Christianity," in Krister Stendahl, ed., *The Scrolls and the New Testament* (New York, 1957), p. 30. Raffael Gyllenberg calls attention to a suggestion made by Bultmann in 1925 that the Johannine tradition might represent a type older than Synoptic Christianity. Herder had mentioned this possibility as early as 1797. Gyllenberg suggests that Johannine Christianity was perhaps one wing of the primitive church, influenced by John the Baptist and located in the Jordan valley, Bethany, Jerusalem, and perhaps also in Cana. John the Baptist worked in the Jordan valley. Jesus goes there. At the Jordan he begins his ministry and gathers his first disciples. From there he takes off on his tours to Jerusalem, Cana and Galilee. If Jesus' public ministry lasted two years, he spent eight to nine months in Galilee, a considerably shorter time in Jerusalem, the remainder in Judea, perhaps mostly in the area of the Jordan. Raffael Gyllenberg, "Die Anfänge der johanneischen Tradition," *Neutestamentliche Studien für Rudolf Bultmann* (Berlin, 1954), pp. 144–147. S. Schulz, "Die Komposition des Johannesprologs und die Zusammensetzung des 4. Evangeliums," *Studia Evangelica* (Berlin, 1959), pp. 351–362, singles out a heterodox, hellenistic, apocalyptic and gnostic background in Judaism. At the core of the Johannine tradition is a *Chaburah*, a communion of converts from Qumran and the Baptist communities, probably priests. The background explains why there is so much opposition in the discourses against official Pharisee Judaism. There existed a pre-Christian, anti-Pharisee and anti-rabbinical Judaism. See also Siegfried Schulz, *Untersuchungen zur Menschensohn-Christologie im Johannesevangelium* (Göttingen, 1957), pp. 175f.

6. Hoskyns, pp. 70, 73.   7. *Ibid.*, p. 126.

8. *Ibid.*, p. 85.   9. *Ibid.*, pp. 81f.

10. *Ibid.*, pp. 84f.   11. *Ibid.*, p. 84.   12. *Ibid.*, p. 116.

13. James M. Robinson, *A New Quest of the Historical Jesus* (Naperville, 1959), pp. 79f.

14. Hoskyns, p. 117.   15. *Ibid.*, pp. 129ff.

16. William Wrede, *Charakter und Tendenz des Johannesevangeliums* (Tübingen, 1933), p. 13, suggests that the prologue (1:1–18) appears to be similar to the discourses of Jesus in the Fourth Gospel. Structurally there is a unity between prologue and discourses. It is possible that the prologue is based on a hymn of a Baptist sect, as Bultmann, *Das Evangelium des Johannes*

(Göttingen, 1950), p. 5, assumes. But that does not disprove its basic similarity with the discourse passages. See also Wilhelm Wilkens, *Die Entstehungsgeschichte des vierten Evangeliums* (Zollikon, 1958), p. 118.

17. Alan Richardson, *The Gospel According to Saint John* (London, 1959), is wrestling throughout his commentary with this issue and offers an excellent example of how theology today might come to grips with it. See especially pp. 26, 58, 64, 79, 80, 88, 89, 91, 113, 117, 120, 128, 135, 160, 164. The principal thought to keep in mind is that it is presenting us "the truth of history in the form of a story." (p. 215)

18. Hoskyns, pp. 136f. Cf. C. H. Dodd, *The Interpretation of the Fourth Gospel* (Cambridge, 1955), p. 284: "Thus not only verses 11–13, but the whole passage from verse 4, is *at once* an account of the relations of the Logos with the world, *and* an account of the ministry of Jesus Christ, which in every essential particular reproduces these relations." Cf. also Rudolf Bultmann, "The Interpretation of the Fourth Gospel," *New Testament Studies* (Vol. I, 1954/55), p. 86. For an alternative view, see Eric Lane Titus, *The Message of the Fourth Gospel* (New York and Nashville, 1957), p. 43. For the problem in the context of an evaluation of the theology of the four Gospels, see Günther Bornkamm, *Jesus of Nazareth* (New York, 1960), p. 189.

19. Ernst Fuchs, *Hermeneutik*, p. 70, gives a most revealing formulation of the problem when he says that the question of God is the complaint about the failure to be able to articulate the word.

20. Hoskyns, p. 139. The concern of the prologue for the relationship between history and Word is at its core a concern for the understanding of God. John Macquarrie, *The Scope of Demythologizing* (New York, 1960), p. 93, relates the prologue to Christian existence: "Talk of 'following Christ' might be just as ridiculous as talk of emulating the feats of Herakles if there were no assurance that the possibility of Christian existence has been fulfilled by someone under the conditions of 'real' life. And we can have reasonable assurance on this point, whatever historical criticism may be saying about the details of the Christian story at any given time. Put into theological language, the minimal assertion is that 'the Word became flesh and dwelt among us', in one possible sense of this pregnant saying." In the present discussion it seems this one possible sense of the saying that the Word became flesh is subject to the understanding of God. The understanding of Christian existence is a *sequel* to the understanding of God. For a critique of the idea that we need an assurance that Christian existence has been fulfilled under the conditions of 'real' life, see Schubert M. Ogden, *Christ Without Myth* (New York, 1961), p. 179.

21. Paul Tillich, *Systematic Theology*, Vol. I (Chicago, 1951), pp. 20f.

22. Paul Tillich, *Biblical Religion and the Search for Ultimate Reality* (Chicago, 1955), pp. 75f.

23. *Ibid.*, p. 79.

24. C. H. Dodd, *The Interpretation of the Fourth Gospel* (Cambridge, 1955), p. 277.

25. *Ibid.*, pp. 177f.

26. For an interpretation in the former direction, see Ernest C. Colwell and Eric L. Titus, *The Gospel of the Spirit* (New York, 1953), pp. 71–83; for the latter tendency, see Rudolf Bultmann, *Theology of the New Testament* (New York, 1955), Vol. 2, pp. 40ff., 50, 62.

27. W. C. van Unnik, "The Purpose of St. John's Gospel," *Studia Evangelica* (Berlin, 1959), pp. 385f.

28. The theory that the Fourth Gospel was written against the Jews helps little for the understanding of its theology. Karl Jaspers, for example, speaks of the first Christian anti-Semitism found in the Fourth Gospel. Karl Jaspers and Rudolf Bultmann, *Myth and Christianity* (New York, 1958), p. 21. Judgments of this type are not infrequent. The main problem can briefly be stated: Since it is likely that the author of the Fourth Gospel was a Jew, how was it possible that a Jew could speak of Jews in such derogatory terms? J. Jocz, "Die Juden und das Johannesevangelium," *Judaica* (9. Jhrg., Heft 3, 1953), pp. 140f., claims that since the book is written in the interest of faith, we must not read modern anti-Semitism into the Gospel. Just because John speaks as a Jew, he feels all the more pain because of the unbelief of his people. Jocz quotes Lord Charnwood as saying that John is "in style and mind an intense Jew. His very anger with his own race is that of a Jew. No Gentile, though he might dislike Jews, would have shown it in the same way; he would have felt, e.g. no interest in shifting more blame on to the Jewish Sanhedrin off the shoulders of Pilate." The view of S. Schulz to which we referred in n. 5 would support the principal point. For a position that suggests a complete break between the author of the Fourth Gospel and the Jews, see Walter Bauer, *Das Johannesevangelium* (Tübingen, 1933), p. 31. Against this interpretation, see van Unnik, p. 407.

29. Van Unnik, p. 391.   30. *Ibid.*, pp. 394, 396f.

31. *Ibid.*, p. 399.   32. *Ibid.*, p. 410.

33. But see C. K. Barrett, *The Gospel According to St. John* (London, 1955), p. 115.

34. J. A. T. Robinson, "The Destination and Purpose of St. John's Gospel," *New Testament Studies* (Vol. 6, 1959), p. 130.

35. A recent work on this line of thought is Wilhelm Wilkens, *Die Entstehungsgeschichte des vierten Evangeliums* (Zollikon, 1958). Wilkens argues that every word and deed of Jesus is made part of the Passion narrative. The cross is central in the Fourth Gospel (p. 171). James M. Robinson, "Recent Research in the Fourth Gospel," *JBL* (Vol. 78, 1959), p. 245, calls

attention to some of the inconsistencies inherent in the thesis. See also C. K. Barrett's review of Wilkens' book in *Theologische Literaturzeitung* (No. 11, 1959), p. 829.

36. Cf. Hans Jonas, "Heidegger and Theology," *The Review of Metaphysics*, 18:2 (December, 1964), p. 217: The "crucifixion . . . was not in the first place an event of language."

37. Van Gogh, *op. cit.*, p. 45.

38. It is of interest to note the concern for Jesus' poetry in such a scholarly study as that of C. F. Burney, *The Poetry of Our Lord* (Oxford, 1925). Cf. William Ellery Leonard, *The Poet of Galilee* (New York, 1928). Both books do not use exactly the same definition of the poetic as we, and Leonard hardly concerns himself with the Fourth Gospel; but both prove that Jesus' word as poetic word deserves more theological consideration than it usually receives.

39. Hoskyns, *op. cit.*, pp. 117, 121.   40. *Ibid.*, p. 136.

41. I am quite aware of the difficulty of using adequate language at this point. In terms of principle I find myself close to the position of Hans Jonas, "Heidegger and Theology," p. 231: "The question is not how to devise an adequate language for theology, but how to keep its necessary inadequacy *transparent* for what is to be indicated by it: its lesser or greater opaqueness is a matter about which something can be done." I especially appeal to his conclusion: "The final paradox is better protected by the symbols of myth than by the concepts of thought. Where the mystery is rightfully at home, 'we see in a glass darkly.' . . . Myth taken *literally* is crudest objectification. Myth taken *allegorically* is sophisticated objectification. Myth taken *symbolically* is the glass through which we darkly see." (pp. 232f.)

42. Hoskyns, p. 129.

43. James M. Robinson and John B. Cobb, Jr., eds., *The New Hermeneutic* (New York, Evanston, and London, 1964), p. 77.

44. From a hymn by William Cowper, No. 75 in *The Hymnal* (Saint Louis, 1941).

45. Jürgen Moltmann, *Theologie der Hoffnung* (München, 1964).

46. For example, see *ibid.*, pp. 250–279.

47. *Ibid.*, pp. 12ff.   48. *Ibid.*, pp. 24ff.   49. *Ibid.*, p. 34.

50. I did consider analyzing other models of New Testament hermeneutic, for example, Romans 1. My primary intention, however, was to examine the Fourth Gospel hermeneutic in view of the growing interest in this gospel in present-day theology. I wished to find out what a responsible hermeneutical appeal to the Fourth Gospel might involve. A turning to other models might have led me to pursue goals I did not set for myself in

conceiving the purpose of the book. So I confined myself, hoping that *less* would be *more*.

51. Jürgen Moltmann, "Anfrage und Kritik: Zu G. Ebelings 'Theologie und Verkündigung,'" *Evangelische Theologie*, 24:1 (January, 1964), pp. 33f.

52. *Ibid.*

CHAPTER IV

1. My translation of the German:
> Schläft ein Lied in allen Dingen,
> die da träumen fort und fort,
> und die Welt hebt an zu singen,
> triffst du nur das Zauberwort.

Eichendorff, *Werke*, Vol. 3 (Tempel Verlag: Berlin, n. d.), p. 495.

2. As to the possibilities of broadening the debate in a Roman Catholic-Protestant dialogue, see James M. Robinson, "Scripture and Theological Method: A Protestant Study in *Sensus Plenior*," *The Catholic Biblical Quarterly*, 27:1 (January, 1965), pp. 6–27.

3. See James M. Robinson and John B. Cobb, Jr., eds., *The Later Heidegger and Theology* (New York, Evanston, and London, 1963), pp. 103ff.

4. James M. Robinson and John B. Cobb, Jr., eds., *The New Hermeneutic* (New York, Evanston, and London, 1964), p. 21 (referred to as *NH* hereinafter).

5. *Ibid.*, p. 39.   6. *Ibid.*, pp. 39, 46f.

7. *Ibid.*, pp. 49f.   8. *Ibid.*, pp. 54, 59.   9. *Ibid.*, p. 143.

10. See Ernst Fuchs, *Hermeneutik* (Bad Cannstadt, 1958), p. 155. In his *Hermeneutik* Fuchs does try to state the question that guides the new hermeneutic. See also pp. 116ff., 122, 125.

11. *NH*, p. 70.   12. *Ibid.*, p. 231.

13. *Ibid.*, pp. 232–243.   14. *Ibid.*, p. 138.

15. *Ibid.*, p. 54.   16. *Ibid.*, p. 141.   17. *Ibid.*, p. 241.

18. Fuchs, *Hermeneutik*, pp. 62, 165. Cf. Ernst Fuchs, *Studies of the Historical Jesus* (London and Naperville, 1964), p. 31: "The quest of the historical Jesus is now essentially transformed into the quest of the reality of the encounter with God in *preaching*."

19. *NH*, p. 144.   20. *Ibid.*, p. 241.   21. *Ibid.*, p. 242.

22. *Ibid.*, p. 55. See also Ernst Fuchs, *Studies of the Historical Jesus*, p. 186: ". . . a hermeneutic of faith, which I understand as faith's 'doctrine of language.'"

23. Gerhard Ebeling, *The Nature of Faith* (Philadelphia, 1961), p. 76.

24. Paul Tillich, *Systematic Theology*, Vol. I (Chicago, 1951), p. 20.

25. See *NH*, p. 55. In a footnote (no. 157) the matter of the relationship between language and reality is taken up. It is regrettable that these reflections were relegated to a footnote and could not be developed further.
For an excellent evaluation of the relationship between language and reality in the new hermeneutic, see Paul J. Achtemeier, "How Adequate Is the New Hermeneutic?" *Theology Today*, 23:1 (April, 1966), pp. 117–119.

26. Gerhard Ebeling in *NH*, p. 96.

27. Frederick Ferré, *Language, Logic and God* (New York, 1961), p. 160. I note the same trend in Ian T. Ramsey, *Christian Discourse: Some Logical Explorations* (London, New York, Toronto, 1965).

28. Ferré, pp. 161, 163.

29. *Ibid.*, p. 164.

30. It might be appropriate to indicate at this point that in our view theological linguistics deals primarily with the use of words in theology, the new hermeneutic with the Word of God, and the hermeneutic of God with the word "God." Theological linguistics and the new hermeneutic perhaps assume that the language *is* the understanding. The hermeneutic of God presupposes that the "Sitz im Leben" of the language has to be taken into account, too.

31. *NH*, p. 62.   32. *Ibid.*, p. 63.

33. *Ibid.*, p. 62.   34. *Ibid.*, p. 77.   35. *Ibid.*, p. 123.

36. For an excellent summary of Bultmann's view of early Christian history, see Rudolf Bultmann, *Jesus and the Word* (New York and London, 1934), pp. 3–15.

37. The reasons for the dilemma we are facing in Bultmann at this point have been superbly analysed by Schubert M. Ogden, "Bultmann's Demythologizing and Hartshorne's Dipolar Theism," in William L. Reese and Eugene Freeman, eds., *Process and Divinity: The Hartshorne Festschrift* (La Salle, 1964), p. 501: "Bultmann presents an anomaly. On the one hand, he clearly does not wish to deny that theology must speak as directly of God as it speaks of man; and he himself not only continually engages in such speaking, but even attempts to justify it by his fragmentary theory of analogy. On the other hand, he so stresses the procedure of existential interpretation as apparently to preclude the very direct speaking of God he has no intention of denying."

38. Rudolf Bultmann, *Existence and Faith* (New York, 1960), p. 108. Cf. Langdon B. Gilkey, "Secularism's Impact on Contemporary Theology," *Christianity and Crisis*, 25:5 (April 5, 1965), p. 65.

39. In an essay which stresses the hermeneutical character of theology, "Theology as Translation," *Theology Today*, 20:4 (January, 1964), pp. 518–527, James M. Robinson raises no questions as regards the validity of God-language. He principally affirms the faith of the Reformation: "God's word remains *ubi et quando visum est Deo*." In his response to the essay by Carl E. Braaten, "How New Is the New Hermeneutic?" *Theology Today*, 22:2 (July, 1965), pp. 218–235, he reaffirms this position in a critical point directed towards Braaten's view of hermeneutic: "Braaten's appeal to the Spirit in speaking about his hermeneutics seems more like a return to 'pneumatic exegesis' than a recognition shared by the new hermeneutic that the hearing of God takes place *ubi et quando visum est Deo*." James M. Robinson, "Braaten's Polemic: A Reply," *Theology Today*, 22:2 (July, 1965), p. 282. One of the purposes of our book is to ask the new hermeneutic whether it would not be possible to examine more fully the *visum est Deo*.

40. Cf. Hans Jonas, "Heidegger and Theology," *The Review of Metaphysics*, 18:2 (December, 1964), p. 219: "My theological friends, my Christian friends—don't you see what you are dealing with? Don't you sense, if not see, the profoundly pagan character of Heidegger's thought? Rightly pagan, insofar as it is philosophy, though not every philosophy must be so devoid of objective norms; but more pagan than others from your point of view, not in spite but because of its, also, speaking of call and self-revealing and even of the shepherd. . . . Apart from the blasphemous ring which this use of the hallowed title must have to Jewish and Christian ears—it is hard to hear man hailed as the shepherd of being when he has just so dismally failed to be his brother's keeper." (p. 229) It is often said by those who use Heidegger in one way or other in their theological enterprise that they use his philosophy in a formal manner only. I do not see how this is possible. Heidegger's concepts predetermine, so it appears to me at least, much more than merely formal ways of assessing things. In terms of *Being and Time*, to use one example, there is no truth beyond man: "Before there was any Dasein, there was no truth; nor will there be any after Dasein is no more. . . . That there are 'eternal truths' will not be adequately proved until someone has succeeded in demonstrating that Dasein has been and will be for all eternity." Martin Heidegger, *Being and Time* (London, 1962), pp. 269f. Would Heidegger's concept of truth have no substantive implications if one, for example, were to use it for the interpretation of truth ("I am . . . the truth") in the Fourth Gospel?

41. The passage we are referring to is part of a somewhat involved argument:

> 'T is written: "In the Beginning was the Word."
> Here am I balked: who, now, can help afford?
> The Word?—impossible so high to rate it;
> And otherwise must I translate it,

If by the Spirit I am truly taught.
Then thus: "In the beginning was the *Thought*."
This first line let me weigh completely,
Lest my impatient pen proceed too fleetly.
Is it the *Thought* which works, creates, indeed?
"In the Beginning was the *Power*," I read.
Yet, as I write, a warning is suggested,
That I the sense may not have fairly tested.
The Spirit aids me: now I see the light!
"In the Beginning was the *Act*," I write.

Johann Wolfgang von Goethe, *Faust*, trans. by Bayard Taylor (New York, 1950), p. 43.

42. *NH*, p. 103.   43. *Ibid.*, p. 100.

44. Ebeling, *The Nature of Faith*, pp. 75f., 81.

45. *Ibid.*, p. 82.

46. Gerhard Ebeling, *Word and Faith* (Philadelphia, 1963), pp. 347, 351.

47. See also the critique of Ebeling from a quite different perspective in Harvey Cox, *The Secular City* (New York, 1965), p. 259: "Such contemporary theologians as Fuchs, Ebeling, and Braun, who are rightly concerned that God not be confused with an object among other objects, have performed an invaluable service to theology. They are justified in emphasizing that there can be no relationship to God which does not include a relationship to man. But it is also true that if God is not an object of man's knowledge or curiosity, He is also not to be identified with some particular quality in man or in human reciprocity, and He is not just a confused mode of speaking about relationships between men." Fuchs and Ebeling hardly wish to speak of God merely in terms of human reciprocity. With Braun it is different.

48. Cf. Paul L. Holmer, "The Logic of Preaching," *Dialog*, 4:3 (Summer, 1965), p. 212; also James T. Cleland, *Preaching to be Understood* (New York and Nashville, 1965), pp. 42ff.

49. *NH*, p. 106.   50. *Ibid.*, p. 107.

51. Cf. Ernst Fuchs, *Hermeneutik*, p. 69: "True language is beautiful. (In this respect the sermon is akin to poetry.)"

52. We are speaking here in terms of analogy, not identity. The word of proclamation does not merely give content to an ontological possibility of man. It draws upon an ontological reality, the reality of God's costly love. But in drawing upon this, it interprets man's experience anew. What we wish to suggest might be understood in contrast to Bultmann's position,

which is that the word of proclamation is only an ontic qualification of man's potential. Cf. Rudolf Bultmann, *Existence and Faith*, pp. 106ff.

53. Enid Welsford, *The Fool: His Social and Literary History* (New York, 1961), pp. 322ff.

54. Johan Huizinga, *Homo Ludens: A Study of the Play-Element in Culture* (Boston, 1955), p. 3.

55. I owe the expression to Martin Fischer, "Die diakonische Predigt," in *Einer trage des Andern Last* (Berlin, 1957), pp. 13–51.

56. The possibility of speaking of diakonic existence came first to my attention in Gerhard Ebeling, *Theologie und Verkündigung* (Tübingen, 1962), p. 5. Cf. Johannes Hoekendijk, *Die Zukunft der Kirche und die Kirche der Zukunft* (Stuttgart and Berlin, 1964), pp. 161–166.

CHAPTER V

1. Norman Cousins, *Dr. Albert Schweitzer of Lambaréné* (New York, 1960), p. 114.

2. John A. T. Robinson, *Honest to God* (Philadelphia, 1963), p. 105.

3. Paul Lehmann, *Ethics in a Christian Context* (New York and Evanston, 1963), p. 24.

4. See Frederick K. Wentz, *The Times Test the Church* (Philadelphia, 1956), p. 197.

5. Reinhold Niebuhr, *An Interpretation of Christian Ethics* (New York, 1958), p. 36.

6. *Ibid.*, p. 54.   7. *Ibid.*, p. 61.

8. *Ibid.*, p. 136.   9. *Ibid.*, pp. 97f., 110.

10. John A. T. Robinson, *Christian Morals Today* (Philadelphia, 1964), p. 33.

11. *Ibid.*, pp. 12f.   12. *Ibid.*, pp. 39, 42.

13. *Ibid.*, p. 26.   14. *Ibid.*, p. 35.   15. *Ibid.*, pp. 18, 20.

16. *Time* (March 5, 1965), pp. 42ff.

17. William Robert Miller, *Nonviolence: A Christian Interpretation* (New York, 1964), p. 18.

18. *Ibid.*, pp. 44f., 55.   19. *Ibid.*, pp. 38f.

20. *Ibid.*, p. 36.   21. *Ibid.*, p. 177.

22. Robert W. Spike, *The Freedom Revolution and the Churches* (New York, 1965), pp. 124f.

23. Gerhard Kittel, ed., *Theologisches Wörterbuch zum Neuen Testament* (Stuttgart, 1949), Vol. I, pp. 36ff.

24. As regards the primitive church, the point has been carefully substantiated by Hendrik Bolkestein, *Wohltätigkeit und Armenpflege im vorchristlichen Altertum* (Utrecht, 1939), in terms of Fénélon's definition: La charité est la philanthropie animée par l'amour de Dieu. See p. 483.

25. Cf. the close relationship Ian T. Ramsey sees between being and love, "On Understanding Mystery," *The Chicago Theological Seminary Register*, 53:5 (May, 1963), p. 9: "So it is with 'loving' or 'being.' Qualifiers have to be added if they are going to take us to God. . . ."

26. Miller, p. 167.

27. *The Saturday Evening Post* (April 10, 1965), p. 10.

28. Harvey Cox, *The Secular City* (New York, 1965), p. 140. Roger L. Shinn, *Tangled World* (New York, 1965), pp. 80f., makes the same point by calling attention to the need for changing institutions. He opposes "the common opinion that hearts must change before institutions can change." In fact, "Institutions can change hearts." True. Only that everything depends on the hearts that change the institutions. The institutions of Nazism also changed hearts. The same is true of the institutions of Communism.

29. Cox, p. 265.

30. The literature in this area is vast. As examples let me mention two significant contributions: as regards the bomb, Robert C. Batchelder, *The Irreversible Decision 1939–1950* (New York, 1961); on war, in the context of our present involvement in Vietnam, Don R. Larson and Arthur Larson, *Vietnam and Beyond* (Durham, 1965). Although not written by theologians, the study has significant theological implications.

31. The importance of the theological implications of the racial issue in the United States is widely seen. But they still have to be made explicit, especially in hermeneutical terms. See, for example, William Hamilton, "The Death of God Theology," *The Christian Scholar*, 48:1 (Spring, 1965), p. 46: "It is not yet clear how the civil rights movement is going to take on its theological significance, but it clearly is beginning to already, as the radical, southern Negro student comes out of the movement to seminary. He brings a passionate interest in the New Testament doctrines of discipleship and following Jesus, for example, and very little interest in the doctrine of sin. One of the most pressing intellectual responsibilities of the Negro student and minister today is that of working out some of the ethical and theological clues that the Negro revolution is teaching him and us all." For an outstanding attempt to think constructively about the subject, see James Sellers, "A Fuller Definition of Civil Rights," in Martin E. Marty and Dean G. Peerman, eds., *New Theology No. 1* (New York and London, 1964),

pp. 219–231. Cf. also William Stringfellow, "Through Dooms of Love," in Martin E. Marty and Dean G. Peerman, eds., *New Theology No. 2* (New York and London, 1965), pp. 288–296.

32. James M. Robinson and John B. Cobb, Jr., eds., *The New Hermeneutic* (New York, Evanston, and London, 1964), p. 135.

33. Cousins, *loc. cit.* The reciprocity between ethics and systematic theology has been keenly focused by James M. Gustafson: "Ethics has a heavy stake in systematic theology. It is not as if a settlement of the questions involved in discussions of God would lead to an automatic fallout of right morals, or even of ethical guidelines. But one's disposition toward the world, his view of the nature and functions of social institutions, and his perspectives on hope and despair are governed to a large degree by basic beliefs." "Christian Faith and Moral Action," *The Christian Century*, 82:44 (November 3, 1965), p. 1347.

34. Paul Ramsey, *Deeds and Rules in Christian Ethics* (Edinburgh and London, 1965), pp. 2f. Cf. the excellent review article by James M. Gustafson, "How Does Love Reign?" *The Christian Century* (May 18, 1966), pp. 654f.

35. Ramsey, pp. 50f.

36. Lehmann, *op. cit.*, p. 160.   37. *Ibid.*, p. 104.

38. God's waiting on man does not mean that he is man's "omnipotent servant." See Will Herberg, *Protestant-Catholic-Jew* (New York, 1956), p. 285. God's *diakonia* in Jesus' cross is not characterized by omnipotence but by lowliness. Man is offended by it. Only if man is renewed by God's Spirit is he willing to accept God's waiting on him.

39. James M. Gustafson, "Context Versus Principles: A Misplaced Debate in Christian Ethics," *Harvard Theological Review*, 82:37 (April, 1965), p. 202.

40. See Ramsey, pp. 100ff.

41. Lehmann, p. 347.

42. For a full discussion of the issue of *diakonia*, see my study, "Diakonia in Modern Times: 18th–20th Centuries," in James I. McCord and T. H. L. Parker, eds., *Service in Christ* (London, 1966), pp. 135–150.

43. James M. Gustafson, "Christian Ethics," in Paul Ramsey, ed., *Religion* (Englewood Cliffs, 1965), p. 287.

44. Cox, *op. cit.*, pp. 125f. Cox too knows of the healing function of the church (see, for example, p. 134). The gambler image, however, introduces a factor that is at cross-purposes with the healing function.

45. *Ibid.*, p. 126.   46. *Ibid.*, p. 141.   47. *Ibid.*

48. *Ibid.*, p. 160. Cox does see the danger of the *ad hoc* congregations. But since he is determined in his reasoning by a contextual ethic, his criticism (cf. pp. 160f.) is not incisive enough.

49. Cf. Elaine and Ronald Mark, "Reaching the Culturally Deprived in the Inner City," *Church School Worker*, 16:5 (January, 1966), pp. 13–15, 30.

50. In his *Situation Ethics* (Philadelphia, 1966), Joseph Fletcher admits the relevance of an appeal to God in Christian ethics. But such an appeal appears to have few practical consequences. He can say: "In Christian ethics it is more than a doctrinaire formality to insist that before we ask the ethical question, 'What shall I do?' comes the *pre*ethical question, 'What has God done?' " (p. 157) I do not find any single instance, however, where this insight is carefully applied. In fact, I find much that seems to contradict it. For example, Fletcher claims: "Augustine asserted that 'you love yourself suitably when you love God more than yourself'. In this formula we can substitute neighbor for God." (p. 111) With this substitution in mind, I can understand why Fletcher early in the book affirms: "The *Christian* is neighbor-centered first and last." (p. 31) In the long run, situation ethics will be unable to avoid assessing more carefully what it means to ask: "What has God done?" Fletcher claims, for example, that we can lovingly tell a lie. (p. 65) But can the Christian ever *lovingly* tell a lie? How can telling a lie ever be a loving response to God's love, to what God has done? We might often be unable to speak the truth; this is never a reflection of God's love, however, but of our own lack of love.

51. In my opinion no one among the younger generation of American theologians has put his finger as clearly as Harvey Cox on the crucial context in which systematic theology must work: social change. His is a supreme intellectual achievement in this respect. My difficulties begin where he systematizes his theology and tends toward making one model exclusive. Let me illustrate with reference to his article on "The Place and Purpose of Theology," *The Christian Century*, 83:1 (January 5, 1966), pp. 7–9. Here he argues that "the purpose of theology is to serve the prophetic community." This means that "the place of theology is that jagged edge where the faithful company grapples with the swiftest currents of the age." From this vantage point he consistently moves toward his final judgment: "The theologian who is not making up his mind at the place where today's new Adams and new Moseses are composing new chapters in the biblical saga is out of place; the purpose he serves is spurious; and his theology will continue to be religious and apolitical. Consequently it will not be prophetic."

But is not the prophetic only *one* facet of New Testament thought? St. Paul can say: "Now you are the body of Christ, and individually members of it. And God has appointed in the church first apostles, second *prophets*, third teachers, then workers of miracles, then healers, helpers, administrators, speakers in various kinds of tongues. Are all apostles? *Are all prophets?* . . . *And if I have prophetic powers,* and understand all mysteries and all knowledge, and if I have all faith, so as to remove mountains, but have not love, I am nothing." (I Cor. 12:27–13:2).

For St. Paul the prophetic obviously was *one* possibility of Christian witness. Does one have to be prophetic if one does not have the charism? Perhaps one could also appeal at this point to the fact that the church has thought of Christ as prophet, *priest and king.* The tradition of the church would not seem to suggest that we should have to pour the whole of Christian life into the prophetic. Moreover, Cox's type of the prophetic borders on the plethoric. New Adams and new Moseses? Why should not one new Adam be enough and one Moses? Finally, why does one have to be so self-conscious about being a prophet? Cox wants to hear and to help his "comrades in the cadre of prophets." Does this not leave out many poor pedestrians who are trudging lonely roads in trying to follow their Master?

52. An excellent study guide in this area is Lyle E. Schaller, *Community Organization: Conflict and Reconciliation* (New York and Nashville, 1966). See also David A. Satten, "West Side Story," *The New Republic,* 155:1 (July 2, 1966), pp. 15–19.

CHAPTER VI

1. Gerhard Ebeling, *Word and Faith* (Philadelphia, 1963), p. 421.

2. If the significance of the texts is denied from the very outset of a theological enterprise, the problem of the task of systematic theology does not even rise to view. See Paul M. van Buren, "Theology in the Context of Culture," *The Christian Century,* 82:14 (April 7, 1965), p. 430: "The issue is not whether certain ideas or certain ways of expressing them are faithful to some inherited standard or ancient text."

3. Ebeling, p. 431.

4. The point can also be argued the way Ebeling does: "Theology, according to its name, has to do with God. But what about the reality of God? We cannot evade this question, if we are in earnest about the self-criticism of theology. For if theology runs away from the question of the reality of God, then it has already surrendered." *Ibid.,* p. 193.

5. David L. Edwards, ed., *The Honest to God Debate* (Philadelphia, 1963), pp. 188f.

6. Carl Michalson, "The Real Presence of the Hidden God," in Paul Ramsey, ed., *Faith and Ethics: The Theology of H. Richard Niebuhr* (New York, 1957), p. 267, claims: "To say that God *is* love is to create an ontology out of the unreflective witness of Christian piety. The ontology is not as innocent as the witness. For when one says 'God *is* love' the consequence of this predication is to say 'God *must* love. It is his *nature* to love.' But love that is natural or essential is necessary or obliged and there-

fore less than love. . . . There is only one thing God *must* be. He must be God." Michalson's point might be considered an important objection. If the statement "God *is* love" were an abstract ontological affirmation, Michalson would be right. In terms of the historical-ontological hermeneutic, however, the "is" in this instance is determined by the history of Jesus. But it does remain an "is." "God *is* love" means God freely chooses again and again to be love. This is what God wants to be for us. God's self-limitation to this choice—to *be* love—is an aspect of his mystery.

The discussion of this point might soon turn out to be crucial in the debate about the new morality. As one reads what Joseph Fletcher has to say on the subject, one might think—at least at first sight—that he is a complete relativist: "I as a nominalistic ethicist take a relativistic and pragmatic view, seeing right or wrong as predicates but not as properties." But as one reads on, one realizes that he has more to say: "Theologically expressed, only with God is love a property. With finite man it is relative and imperfect and contingent, depending for its measure upon the interplay of motive or intention and the *Gestalt* or configuration of situational factors." Joseph Fletcher, "Agreement and Disagreement," *Commonweal*, 83:14 (January 14, 1966), pp. 438f. The fact that even for Fletcher God's love is a property might be a starting point for moving the debate on. The Christian ethic cannot make that sharp a distinction between God's love and man's love. Otherwise it would be forced into an absolute dualism. St. Paul could say: "God's love has been poured into our hearts through the Holy Spirit which has been given us." (Rom. 5:5) In view of this spiritual reality the problem of the Christian ethic is not to determine how one can translate relative human love into finite situations, but how to translate God's love into human finitude.

7. Harvey Cox, *The Secular City* (New York, 1965), pp. 8of.

8. *Ibid.*, pp. 26of.

9. Ebeling, p. 431.   10. *Ibid.*, p. 432.

11. Thomas J. J. Altizer, "Creative Negation in Theology," *The Christian Century*, 82:27 (July 7, 1965), pp. 864–867.

12. *Ibid.* Altizer is quite aware of the systematic problem involved. See his article, "Theology and the Death of God," *The Centennial Review*, 8:2 (Spring, 1964), p. 129, where he speaks of the crisis of theology "in the relation of dogmatic theology to its biblical ground."

13. Altizer himself speaks of *primal* Christian categories. See Thomas J. J. Altizer, "Nirvana and the Kingdom of God," in Martin E. Marty and Dean G. Peerman (eds.), *New Theology No. 1* (New York and London, 1964), p. 162.

14. Cf. James M. Robinson, "Scripture and Theological Method: A Protestant Study in *Sensus Plenior*," *The Catholic Biblical Quarterly*, 27:1

(January, 1965), p. 26: "The separation of time is an ontological factor in the hermeneutical situation that cannot be bypassed by an appeal to 'contemporaneity' or the creative 'reproduction' of the author's experience in romantic immediacy." From the viewpoint of systematic theology one would wish to say that one indeed understands quite differently today, but still on the basis of an *ontological continuity*. The continuity within the difference is reflected in our approach in the concept of God's Wordpresence.

15. Altizer, "Creative Negation in Theology," p. 866.

16. Altizer, "Nirvana and the Kingdom of God," pp. 162f.

17. In a review of Altizer's book, *Mircea Eliade and the Dialectic of the Sacred*, John E. Skinner has tried to think through the consequences of a consistent death of God theology: "Altizer asks: 'Will the death of God make possible a true resurrection of Jesus? Is Zarathustra the resurrected Jesus?' And he answers his own question with a most curious statement: 'Surely it cannot be an accident that less than a year after writing *The AntiChrist*, when insanity was bursting upon him, Nietzsche could alternately sign his notes "Dionysus" and "The Crucified." ' Does Professor Altizer mean to imply that the mad German is the true Jesus?" *The Witness*, 50:39 (December 2, 1965), p. 11.

18. Especially when the position is stated in popular form, one notices the absence of hermeneutical articulateness. Cf. Ved Mehta, "The New Theologian," *The New Yorker* (November 13, 1965), pp. 142ff. The first clarification of the hermeneutical principle of the death of God theology that has come to my attention is found in Thomas J. J. Altizer, *The Gospel of Christian Atheism* (Philadelphia, 1966), pp. 27f.

19. Cf. the critique of present-day systematic theology by Ninian Smart, "The Intellectual Crisis of British Christianity," *Theology*, 65 (January, 1965), pp. 31–38. Note the sigh: "From being, bliks, Braithwaite and van Buren, good Lord deliver us. From 'I'm I', alleged logical oddity and penny-dropping, good universe-coming-alive-in-a-personal-way deliver us. From looking on freedom as a mere contagion, good affirmative-attitude deliver us."

20. Carl Michalson, "The Task of Systematic Theology Today," *The Centennial Review*, 8:2 (Spring, 1964), pp. 189–199.

21. *Ibid.*, p. 190.

22. Rudolf Bultmann, "Der Gottesgedanke und der moderne Mensch," *Zeitschrift für Theologie und Kirche*, 60:3 (December, 1963), pp. 335–348. Note especially the parallel (though qualified) Bultmann sees between his own position and that of Troeltsch.

23. Since the hermeneutical effort deals with matters that seem to raise little question for many, it is frequently regarded as superfluous. It is actually very much compelled to deal with "doctrines felt as facts" or "the premises

which are never mentioned." As regards these doctrines or premises see Arnold Nash, *The University and the Modern World* (London, 1945), p. 36.

24. See Wolf-Dieter Marsch, *Gegenwart Christi in der Gesellschaft* (München, 1965), pp. 236–305.

25. Ebeling, *op. cit.*, p. 421.

BIBLIOGRAPHY
AND INDEX OF NAMES

The bibliography records mainly titles that reflect the great theological conversation now in progress. I sought to include such publications as interconnect either in terms of content or explicit cross-referencing. Obviously every selection will be somewhat arbitrary. My students in a course on contemporary systematic theology used the substance of this bibliography as the basis of their own bibliographical research and wrote papers on the present theological debate in the following areas: (1) Nonreligious Theology, (2) Social Change Theology, (3) Hermeneutic Theology, (4) Linguistic Theology, (5) Christian Natural Theology, (6) Revelation Theology, (7) Death of God Theology. With the inclusion of the bibliography in this book I am expressing the hope that it might prove similarly useful in other courses on contemporary theology.

Achtemeier, Paul J. "How Adequate is the New Hermeneutic?" *Theology Today* (April, 1966).

Altizer, Thomas J. J. *The Gospel of Christian Atheism* (Philadelphia, 1966).

————. *Mircea Eliade and the Dialectic of the Sacred* (Philadelphia, 1963).

————. *Oriental Mysticism and Biblical Eschatology* (Philadelphia, 1961).

————. "Creative Negation in Theology," *The Christian Century* (July 7, 1965).

————. "The Death of God: Is This Our Situation?" *Christian Advocate* (October 7, 1965).

Altizer, Thomas J. J., and Hamilton, William. *Radical Theology and the Death of God* (Indianapolis, 1966).

Anderson, Hugh. *Jesus and Christian Origins* (New York, 1964).

Armstrong, C. B. "Christianity Without Religion," in *New Theology No. 2.*

Bennett, John C. "In Defense of God," *Look* (April 19, 1966).

Berger, Elmer. "On the 'Death of God' Theologies," *Education in Judaism* (January, 1966).

Berton, Pierre. *The Comfortable Pew: A Critical Look at Christianity and the Religious Establishment in the New Age* (Philadelphia, 1965).

Besson, Waldemar, ed. *Geschichte* (Frankfurt, 1961).

Bochenski, Joseph M. *The Logic of Religion* (New York, 1965).

Bouquet, A. C. "Immanence in Christian Theology," *Religion in Life* (Winter, 1963–1964).

Braaten, Carl E. "The Current Controversy on Revelation: Pannenberg and His Critics," *The Journal of Religion* (July, 1965).

———. "How New Is the New Hermeneutic?" *Theology Today* (July, 1965).

———. "The Quest for True Authority," *The Lutheran Quarterly* (February, 1965).

Braaten, Carl E., and Harrisville, Roy A., eds. *The Historical Jesus and the Kerygmatic Christ* (Nashville, 1964).

Braun, Herbert. *Gesammelte Studien zum Neuen Testament* (Tübingen, 1962).

Brown, James. *Subject and Object in Modern Theology* (New York, 1955).

Brown, Norman O. *Life Against Death: The Psychoanalytical Meaning of History* (Middletown, 1959).

Brown, Raymond E. "After Bultmann What?" *The Catholic Biblical Quarterly* (January, 1964).

Brown, Robert McAfee. *The Spirit of Protestantism* (New York, 1961).

———. "A Campaign on Many Fronts," *The Christian Century* (May 5, 1965).

Buber, Martin. *Eclipse of God* (New York, 1952).

Bultmann, Rudolf. "The Idea of God and Modern Man," *Journal for Theology and the Church*, Vol. 2 (New York, 1965).

———. "Ist der Glaube an Gott erledigt?" *Die Zeit* (May 10, 1963).

———. "On the Question of a Philosophical Theology," *Union Seminary Quarterly Review* (March, 1965).

———. "What Sense Is There To Speak of God?" *The Christian Scholar* (Fall, 1960).

Buri, Fritz. "Das Problem des ungegenständlichen Denkens und Redens in der heutigen Theologie," *Zeitschrift für Theologie und Kirche* (November, 1964), pp. 353–371.

Cahill, Joseph P., S. J. "Rudolf Bultmann and Post-Bultmann Tendencies," *The Catholic Biblical Quarterly* (April, 1964). Also published in *New Theology No. 2*.

Callahan, Daniel. "The Secular City: Toward a Theology of Secularity," *Commonweal* (September 17, 1965).

Christian, William A. *Meaning and Truth in Religion* (Princeton, 1964).

————. "The Concept of God as a Derivative Notion," in William L. Reese and Eugene Freeman, eds., *Process and Divinity: The Hartshorne Festschrift* (La Salle, 1964), pp. 181–203.

Cobb, John B., Jr. *A Christian Natural Theology* (Philadelphia, 1965).

————. "Christian Natural Theology and Christian Existence," *The Christian Century* (March 3, 1965).

————. "From Crisis Theology to the Post-Modern World," *The Centennial Review* (Spring, 1964).

————. "A New Trio Arises in Europe," in *New Theology No. 2.*

————. "Whitehead's Philosophy and a Christian Doctrine of Man," *The Journal of Bible and Religion* (July, 1964).

Cox, Harvey. *God's Revolution and Man's Responsibility* (Valley Forge, 1965).

————. *The Secular City* (New York, 1965).

————. "Beyond Bonhoeffer?" *Commonweal* (September 17, 1965).

————. "Cox on His Critics," *Christianity and Crisis* (December 13, 1965).

————. "The Place and Purpose of Theology," *The Christian Century* (January 5, 1966).

————. "The Playboy and the Christian, II," *Theology Today* (January, 1966).

————. "Sociology in a Post-Religious Era," *The Christian Scholar* (Spring, 1965).

Earle, William. "The Paradox and Death of God," in John Wild, ed., *Christianity and Existentialism* (Evanston, 1963), pp. 66–87.

Ebeling, Gerhard. *The Nature of Faith* (Philadelphia, 1961).

————. *Theologie und Verkündigung* (Tübingen, 1962).

————. *Word and Faith* (Philadelphia, 1963).

————. "Existenz zwischen Gott und Gott," *Zeitschrift für Theologie und Kirche* (May, 1965), pp. 86–113.

————. "Der hermeneutische Ort der Gotteslehre bei Petrus Lombardus und Thomas von Aquin," *Zeitschrift für Theologie und Kirche* (November, 1964), pp. 283–326.

————. "The New Hermeneutics and the Early Luther," *Theology Today* (April, 1964).

Edie, James M. "The Absence of God," in John Wild, ed., *Christianity and Existentialism* (Evanston, 1963), pp. 113–148.

Edwards, David L., ed. *The Honest to God Debate* (Philadelphia, 1963).

Ehrhardt, Arnold T. "In Common Honesty," *Scottish Journal of Theology* (December, 1964).

Fackre, Gabriel J. "The Death and Life of God," *Theology and Life* (Fall, 1965).

————. "Secular Theology in the Church," *Minister's Quarterly* (Winter, 1965–1966).

Fairweather, Eugene R. "Christianity and the Supernatural," in *New Theology No. 1.*

Farrer, Austin. *God Is Not Dead* (New York, 1966).

Fennell, William O. "The Theology of True Secularity," in *New Theology No. 2.*

Ferré, Frederick. *Language, Logic and God* (New York, 1961).

————. "A Crisis Déjà Vue?" *The Centennial Review* (Spring, 1964).

Fletcher, Joseph. *Situation Ethics* (Philadelphia, 1966).

————. "Agreement and Disagreement," *Commonweal* (January 14, 1966).

————. "Love Is the Only Measure," *Commonweal* (January 14, 1966).

Flew, Antony and MacIntyre, Alasdair, eds. *New Essays in Philosophical Theology* (London, 1955).

Fuchs, Ernst. *Studies of the Historical Jesus* (Naperville, 1964).

————. "Proclamation and Speech-Event," *Theology Today* (October, 1962).

Funk, Robert W. "Colloquium on Hermeneutics," *Theology Today* (October, 1964).

————. "Logic and the Logos," *The Christian Century* (September 23, 1964).

Gadamer, Hans-Georg. *Wahrheit und Methode* (Tübingen, 1960).

Gardiner, Patrick, ed. *Theories of History* (Glencoe, 1959).

Gerhardsson, Birger. *Memory and Manuscript* (Uppsala, 1961).

Gilkey, Langdon B. *Maker of Heaven and Earth* (New York, 1959).

————. "Dissolution and Reconstruction in Theology," *The Christian Century* (February 3, 1965).

————. "Is God Dead?" and "God Is Not Dead," *Bulletin of Crozer Theological Seminary* (January, 1965).

————. "A New Linguistic Madness," in *New Theology No. 2.*

————. "Secularism's Impact on Contemporary Theology," *Christianity and Crisis* (April 5, 1965).

Gleason, Robert, S. J. *The Search for God* (New York, 1964).

————. "Situational Morality," *Thought* (Winter, 1957–1958).

Gollwitzer, Helmut. *The Existence of God as Confessed by Faith* (Philadelphia, 1965).

Grant, Robert M. "The Study of Early Christianity," in Paul Ramsey, ed., *Religion* (Englewood Cliffs, 1965), pp. 111–154.

Gustafson, James M. "Christian Ethics," in Paul Ramsey, ed., *Religion* (Englewood Cliffs, 1965), pp. 285–354.

————. "Christian Faith and Moral Action," *The Christian Century* (November 3, 1965).

————. "Context Versus Principles: A Misplaced Debate in Christian Ethics," *Harvard Theological Review* (April, 1965).

————. "Theology and Ethics," in Daniel T. Jenkins, ed., *The Scope of Theology* (Cleveland, 1965), pp. 111–132.

Habgood, J. S. *Truths in Tension* (New York, 1965).

————. "The Uneasy Truce Between Science and Theology," in A. R. Vidler, ed., *Soundings: Essays Concerning Christian Understanding* (Cambridge, 1963), pp. 21–41.

Hamilton, Kenneth M. *Revolt Against Heaven* (Grand Rapids, 1965).

————. *God Is Dead: The Anatomy of a Slogan* (Grand Rapids, 1966).

————. "Verifiable Christianity: From Arnold to Van Buren," *Canadian Journal of Theology* (July, 1965).

Hamilton, William. *The New Essence of Christianity* (New York, 1961).

————. "The Death of God Theology," *The Christian Scholar* (Spring, 1965).

————. "The Playboy," *Theology Today* (October, 1965).

————. "The Shape of a Radical Theology," *The Christian Century* (October 6, 1965).

Hammarskjöld, Dag. *Markings* (New York, 1964).

Haroutunian, Joseph. *God With Us* (Philadelphia, 1965).

————. "Theology and American Experience," *Dialog* (Summer, 1965).

Harris, T. George. "The Battle of the Bible," *Look* (July 27, 1965).

Hartshorne, Charles. *The Logic of Perfection* (La Salle, 1962).

————. "Abstract and Concrete Approaches to Deity," *Union Seminary Quarterly Review* (March, 1965).

Harvey, Van A. *The Historian and the Believer* (New York, 1966).

————. "The Historical Jesus, the Kerygma, and the Christian Faith," *Religion in Life* (Summer, 1964).

————. "The Nature and Function of Faith," *The Christian Century* (August 4, 1965).

Hazelton, Roger. "The Future of God," *Andover Newton Quarterly* (January, 1966).

Heidegger, Martin. *Unterwegs zur Sprache* (Pfullingen, 1959).

Hepburn, Ronald W. *Christianity and Paradox* (New York, 1958).

Herberg, Will. "Five Meanings of the Word 'Historical'," *The Christian Scholar* (Winter, 1964).

Hick, John, ed. *The Existence of God* (New York, 1964).

Hodgson, Leonard. "The Word 'God'," *Canadian Journal of Theology* (April, 1965).

Hoekendijk, Johannes Christiaan. *The Church Inside Out* (London, 1966).

Holcomb, Harmon R. "Christianity Without God: A Critical Review of 'The Secular Meaning of the Gospel'," *Foundations* (January, 1965).

Holland, J. A.B. "The Debate about *Honest to God*," *Scottish Journal of Theology* (September, 1964).

Holmer, Paul L. "Contra the New Theologies," *The Christian Century* (March 17, 1965).

————. "Language and Theology," *Harvard Theological Review* (July 1965).

————. "The Logic of Preaching," *Dialog* (Summer, 1965).

————. "Metaphysics and Theology: The Foundations of Theology," *The Lutheran Quarterly* (November, 1965).

————. Paul Tillich and the Language about God," *The Journal of Religious Thought* (1965–1966).

————. "Theology and Belief," *Theology Today* (October, 1965).

Homrighausen, E. G. "The City: God's Gift or Man's Enemy?" *Theology Today* (July, 1965).

Hordern, William. *Speaking of God: The Nature and Purpose of Theological Language* (New York, 1964).

————. "Response to Albert Anderson's Review," *Dialog* (Summer, 1965).

Hübner, Eberhard. "Credo in Deum Patrem?" *Evangelische Theologie*, (December, 1963), pp. 646–672.

Jenkins, Daniel T., ed. *The Scope of Theology* (Cleveland, 1965); chapter on "Systematic Theology," pp. 96–110.

Jenkins, David. "Whither the Doctrine of God Now?" in *New Theology No. 2.*

———. *Guide To the Debate About God* (Philadelphia, 1966).

Johnson, Robert C. "Who Is Heinrich Ott?" in *New Theology No. 1.*

Jonas, Hans. "Heidegger and Theology," *The Review of Metaphysics* (December, 1964).

———. "Immortality and the Modern Temper," *Harvard Theological Review* (January, 1962).

Jüngel, Eberhard. *Gottes Sein ist im Werden* (Tübingen, 1965).

Käsemann, Ernst. *Essays on New Testament Themes* (Naperville, 1964).

Kaufman, Gordon D. "On the Meaning of 'God': Transcendence without Mythology," *The Harvard Theological Review*, 59:2 (April, 1966).

Kegley, Charles W. *Protestantism In Transition* (New York, 1965).

Kelly, Alden D. "On Being a Christian in the World," *Religion in Life* (Winter, 1963–1964).

Knox, John. *The Church and the Reality of Christ* (New York, 1962).

Kümmel, Werner Georg. "Jesusforschung seit 1950," *Theologische Rundschau*, 31:1 (January, 1966), pp. 15–46.

Landon, Harold R., ed. *Reinhold Niebuhr: A Prophetic Voice in Our Time* (Greenwich, 1962).

Larsson, Edvin. *Christus als Vorbild* (Uppsala, 1962).

Lehmann, Paul. *Ethics in a Christian Context* (New York, 1963).

———. "Chalcedon in Technopolis," *Christianity and Crisis* (July 12, 1965).

———. "The Tri-unity of God," *Union Seminary Quarterly Review* (November, 1965).

Lewis, Harland G. "An Honest to God Reformation," *The Christian Century* (June 3, 1964).

Little, David. "The Social Gospel Revisited," *Christianity and Crisis* (July 12, 1965).

MacIntyre, Alasdair, ed. *Difficulties in Christian Belief* (London, 1959).

———. *Metaphysical Beliefs* (London, 1957).

———. "God and the Theologians," in David L. Edwards, ed., *The Honest to God Debate* (Philadelphia, 1963), pp. 215–228.

MacLeish, Archibald. *J. B.* (Boston, 1957).

Macquarrie, John. *Principles of Christian Theology* (New York, 1966).

———. *The Scope of Demythologizing* (New York, 1960).

———. "How Can We Think of God?" *Theology Today* (July, 1965).

———. "How Is Theology Possible?" in *New Theology No. 1*.

Marsch, Wolf-Dieter, *Gegenwart Christi in der Gesellschaft* (München, 1965).

Marty, Martin E., and Peerman, Dean G., eds. *New Theology No. 1* (New York and London, 1964).

———. *New Theology No. 2* (New York and London, 1965).

———. *New Theology No. 3* (New York and London, 1966).

Matson, Wallace I. *The Existence of God* (Ithaca, 1965).

McArthur, Harvey K. "A Survey of Recent Gospel Research," in *New Theology No. 2*.

McCabe, Herbert, O. P. "The Total Context," *Commonweal* (January 14, 1966).

———. "The Validity of Absolutes," *Commonweal* (January 14, 1966).

Mehta, Ved. "The New Theologian," *The New Yorker* (November 13, 20, 27, 1965).

Meland, Bernard E. "Alternatives to Absolutes," *Religion in Life* (Summer, 1965).

———. "A Critique of Haroutunian's Paper on 'Theology and the American Experience'," *Dialog* (Summer, 1965).

———. "A Voice of Candor," *Religion in Life* (Winter, 1963–1964).

Meyerhoff, Hans, ed. *The Philosophy of History in Our Time* (New York, 1959).

Michalson, Carl. *The Rationality of Faith* (New York, 1963).

———. "The Ghost of Logical Positivism," *The Christian Scholar* (Fall, 1960).

———. "The Real Presence of the Hidden God," in Paul Ramsey, ed., *Faith and Ethics: The Theology of H. Richard Niebuhr* (New York, 1957), pp. 245–267.

———. "The Task of Systematic Theology Today," *The Centennial Review* (Spring, 1964).

Miles, T. R. *Religion and the Scientific Outlook* (New York, 1959).

Miller, William Robert. *Nonviolence: A Christian Interpretation* (New York, 1964).

Miskotte, Kornelius Heiko. *Wenn die Götter schweigen* (München, 1963).

Moltmann, Jürgen. *Herrschaft Christi und soziale Wirklichkeit nach Dietrich Bonhoeffer* (München, 1959).

————. *Theologie der Hoffnung* (München, 1964).

————. "Anfrage und Kritik: Zu G. Ebelings 'Theologie und Verkündigung,' " *Evangelische Theologie* (January, 1964), pp. 25–34.

————. "Das 'Prinzip Hoffnung' und die christliche Zuversicht," *Evangelische Theologie* (October, 1963), pp. 537–557.

————. "Exegese und Eschatologie der Geschichte," *Evangelische Theologie* (January–February, 1962), pp. 31–66.

Mondin, Battista, S. X. *The Principle of Analogy in Protestant and Catholic Theology* (The Hague, 1963).

Murray, John Courtney, S. J. *The Problem of God* (New Haven, 1964).

Narot, David J. "Toward a New Theology?" *Yale Alumni Magazine* (December, 1965).

New Theology No. 1 and *No. 2*. See Marty, Martin.

Niebuhr, Reinhold. "Faith as the Sense of Meaning in Human Existence," *Christianity and Crisis* (June 13, 1966).

Niebuhr, Richard R. *Schleiermacher on Christ and Religion* (New York, 1964).

Nielsen, Charles M. "The Loneliness of Protestantism," *The Christian Century* (September 15, 1965).

Nielsen, Kai. "Can Faith Validate God-Talk?" *New Theology No. 1*.

————. "God and the Good: Does Morality Need Religion?" *Theology Today* (April, 1964).

————. "God and Verification Again," *Canadian Journal of Theology* (April, 1965).

Norton–Taylor, Duncan. "What on Earth Is Happening to Protestantism," *Fortune* (December, 1965).

Novak, Michael. "Secular Style and Natural Law," *Christianity and Crisis* (July 26, 1965).

Ogden, Schubert M. *Christ Without Myth* (New York, 1961).

————. "Beyond Supernaturalism," *Religion in Life* (Winter, 1963–1964).

————. "Bultmann's Demythologizing and Hartshorne's Dipolar Theism," in William L. Reese and Eugene Freeman, eds., *Process and Divinity: The Hartshorne Festschrift* (La Salle, 1964), pp. 493–513.

————. "The Christian and Unbelievers," *Motive* (May, 1965).

————. "Faith and Truth," *The Christian Century* (September 1, 1965).

————. "The Possibility and Task of Philosophical Theology," *Union Seminary Quarterly Review* (March, 1965).

————. "Theology and Objectivity," *The Journal of Religion* (July, 1965).

————. "Theology and Philosophy: A New Phase of the Discussion," *The Journal of Religion* (January, 1964).

————. "Welch's Polemic: A Reply," *Theology Today* (July, 1965).

————. "What Sense Does It Make to Say, 'God Acts in History'?" *The Journal of Religion* (January, 1963).

Ogletree, Thomas W. *The Death of God Controversy* (New York and Nashville, 1966).

Ott, Heinrich. *Denken und Sein* (Zollikon–Zürich, 1959).

————. *Theology and Preaching* (Philadelphia, 1965).

————. "Das Problem des nicht-objektivierenden Denkens und Redens in der Theologie," *Zeitschrift für Theologie und Kirche* (November, 1964), pp. 327–352.

————. "The Historical Jesus and the Ontology of History," in Carl E. Braaten and Roy A. Harrisville, eds., *The Historical Jesus and the Kerygmatic Christ* (Nashville, 1964), pp. 142–171.

Pannenberg, Wolfhart. *Grundzüge der Christologie* (Gütersloh, 1964).

————, ed. *Offenbarung als Geschichte* (Göttingen, 1963).

————. "Analogie und Doxologie," in Wilfried Joest und Wolfhart Pannenberg, eds., *Dogma und Denkstrukturen* (Göttingen, 1963), pp. 96–115.

————. "Die Frage nach Gott," *Evangelische Theologie* (April–May, 1965), pp. 238–262.

————. "Einsicht und Glaube," *Theologische Literaturzeitung* (February, 1963), pp. 82–92.

————. "Hermeneutik und Universalgeschichte," *Zeitschrift für Theologie und Kirche* (August, 1963), pp. 90–121.

————. "Redemptive Event and History," in Claus Westermann, ed., *Essays on Old Testament Hermeneutics* (Richmond, 1963), pp. 314–335.

Pike, James A. *What Is This Treasure* (New York, 1966).

Polanyi, Michael. *Personal Knowledge* (Chicago, 1958).

"Protestantism: Mid-Decade Assessment," *The Christian Century* (January 19, 1966).

"The Pursuit of Novelty," *Christianity Today* (March 4, 1966).

Ramsey, Ian T. *Models and Mystery* (New York, 1964).

————. *Religious Language* (New York, 1963).

————, ed. *Prospect for Metaphysics* (London, 1961).

————. "Contemporary Empiricism," *The Christian Scholar* (Fall, 1960).

————. "On Being Articulate about the Gospel," *The Chicago Theological Seminary Register* (May, 1963).

————. "On Understanding Mystery," *The Chicago Theological Seminary Register* (May, 1963).

Ramsey, Paul, ed. *Religion* (Englewood Cliffs, 1965).

————. *Deeds and Rules in Christian Ethics* (Edinburgh, 1965).

Robinson, James M. *A New Quest of the Historical Jesus* (Naperville, 1959).

————. "Braaten's Polemic: A Reply," *Theology Today* (July, 1965).

————. "The Formal Structure of Jesus' Message," in William Klassen and Graydon F. Snyder, eds., *Current Issues in New Testament Interpretation* (New York, 1962).

————. "The Historicality of Biblical Language," in Bernard W. Anderson, ed., *The Old Testament and Christian Faith* (New York, 1963), pp. 124–158.

————. "Scripture and Theological Method; A Protestant Study in *Sensus Plenoir*," *The Catholic Biblical Quarterly* (January, 1965).

————. "Theology as Translation," *Theology Today* (January, 1964).

Robinson, James M., and Cobb, John B., Jr., eds. *The Later Heidegger and Theology* (New York, 1963).

————. *The New Hermeneutic* (New York, 1964).

Robinson, John A. T. *Christian Morals Today* (Philadelphia, 1964).

————. *Honest to God* (Philadelphia, 1963).

————. *The New Reformation?* (Philadelphia, 1965).

Root, H. E. "Beginning All Over Again," in A. R. Vidler, ed., *Soundings: Essays Concerning Christian Understanding* (Cambridge, 1963), pp. 1–19.

Sanders, James Alvin. "The Vitality of the Old Testament: Three Theses," *Union Seminary Quarterly Review* (January, 1966).

Schaller, Lyle E. *Community Organization: Conflict and Reconciliation* (New York and Nashville, 1966).

Schilling, S. Paul. *Contemporary Continental Theologians* (Nashville, 1966).

Schulze, Rudolf. "Hauptlinien der Bonhoeffer-Interpretation," *Evangelische Theologie* (December, 1965), pp. 681–700.

Schweizer, Eduard. "The Relation of Scripture, Church Tradition and Modern Interpretation," in *New Theology No. 1*.

———. "Was heisst 'Gott'?" *Evangelische Theologie* (July, 1965), pp. 339–349.

Scott, Charles E. "Ott's View of Faith Alone," *Religion in Life* (Summer, 1965).

Seils, Martin. "Zur Sprachphilosophischen und Worttheologischen Auseinandersetzung zwischen Existenztheologie und Geschichtstheologie," *Neue Zeitschrift für Systematische Theologie* (1965), pp. 1–14.

"The Servant Church," *Time* (December 25, 1964).

"Shadows of the Antichrist in the Decline of Western Theism," *Christianity Today* (December 17, 1965).

Shinn, Roger L. *Tangled World* (New York, 1965).

———. "Living in a World That Won't Stand Still," *Motive* (October, 1965).

Smart, Ninian. "Being and the Bible," *The Review of Metaphysics* (June, 1956).

———. "The Intellectual Crisis of British Christianity," *Theology* (January, 1965).

———. "The Relation Between Christianity and the Other Great Religions," in A. R. Vidler, ed., *Soundings: Essays Concerning Christian Understanding* (Cambridge, 1963), pp. 103–121.

———. "Theology and Other Religions," in Daniel T. Jenkins, ed., *The Scope of Theology* (Cleveland, 1965), pp. 253–268.

Smith, John E. "Philosophy of Religion," in Paul Ramsey, ed., *Religion* (Englewood Cliffs, 1965), pp. 355–450.

Smith, Ronald Gregor. *The New Man: Christianity and Man's Coming of Age* (New York, 1956).

Steiger, Lothar. *Die Hermeneutik als dogmatisches Problem* (Gütersloh, 1961).

Stern, Fritz, ed. *The Varieties of History* (Cleveland, 1956).

Sturm, Douglas. "Naturalism, Historicism, and Christian Ethics: Toward a Christian Doctrine of Natural Law," *The Journal of Religion* (January, 1964).

Szczesny, Gerhard. *The Future of Unbelief* (New York, 1961).

Thielicke, Helmut. *The Silence of God* (Grand Rapids, 1962).

Tillich, Paul. *The Future of Religions* (New York, 1966).

Torrance, T. F. *Theology in Reconstruction* (Grand Rapids, 1966).

"Toward A Hidden God," *Time* (April 8, 1966).

Tyson, Ruel. "Philosophical Analysis and Religious Language: A Selected Bibliography," *The Christian Scholar* (Fall, 1960).

"U. S. Protestantism: Time for a Second Reformation," *Newsweek* (January 3, 1966).

Vahanian, Gabriel. *The Death of God* (New York, 1961).

———. *Wait Without Idols* (New York, 1964).

———. "Beyond the Death of God: The Need of Cultural Revolution," *Dialog* (Autumn, 1962).

———. "The Future of Christianity in a Post-Christian Era," *The Centennial Review* (Spring, 1964).

Van Buren, Paul M. *The Secular Meaning of the Gospel* (New York, 1964).

———. "The Dissolution of the Absolute," *Religion in Life* (Summer, 1965).

———. "Theology in the Context of Culture," *The Christian Century* (April 7, 1965).

Van den Heuvel, Albert H. "The Honest to God Debate in Ecumenical Perspective," *The Ecumenical Review* (April, 1964).

———. "Secularization as Freedom and Yoke," *Study Encounter* (1965).

Van Leeuwen, Arend Th. *Christianity in World History* (New York, 1966).

Vidler, A. R., ed. *Objections to Christian Belief* (Philadelphia, 1964).

———, ed. *Soundings: Essays Concerning Christian Understanding* (Cambridge, 1963).

Wall, James M. "What Do They Mean, 'God Is Dead'?" *Together* (June, 1966).

Watts, Alan. *Beyond Theology: The Art of Godmanship* (New York, 1964).

Weigel, Gustave, S. J. *The Modern God* (New York, 1963).

Weiss, Paul. *The God We Seek* (Carbondale, 1964).

Welch, Claude. "On Theological Typology," *Theology Today* (July, 1965).

———. "Theology," in Paul Ramsey, ed., *Religion* (Englewood Cliffs, 1965), pp. 218–284.

———. "Theology as Risk," *The Christian Century* (June 2, 1965).

West, Charles C. "What It Means To Be Secular," *Christianity and Crisis* (July 12, 1965).

Westermann, Claus, ed. *Essays on Old Testament Hermeneutics* (Richmond, 1963).

Whitman, Ardis. "The 'God Is Dead' Debate," *Redbook* (June, 1966).

Wilder, Amos. "New Testament Hermeneutics Today," in William Klassen and Graydon F. Snyder, eds., *Current Issues in New Testament Interpretation* (New York, 1962), pp. 38–52.

Williams, Daniel Day. "How Does God Act? An Essay in Whitehead's Metaphysics," in William L. Reese and Eugene Freeman, eds., *Process and Divinity: The Hartshorne Festschrift* (La Salle, 1964), pp. 161–180.

Winter, Gibson. *The New Creation as Metropolis* (New York, 1963).

———. "Theology and Social Science," in Daniel T. Jenkins, ed., *The Scope of Theology* (Cleveland, 1965), pp. 174–198.

———. "A Theology of Demonstration," *The Christian Century* (October 13, 1965).

Wisdom, John. "Gods," in Antony Flew, ed., *Language and Logic* (Garden City, 1960).

———. "The Modes of Thought and the Logic of God," in John Hick, ed., *The Existence of God* (New York, 1964), pp. 275–298.

Woelfel, James W. " 'Non-Metaphysical' Christian Philosophy and Linguistic Philosophy," in *New Theology No. 2*.

Wolf, Donald J., S. J., and James V. Schall, S. J., eds. *Current Trends in Theology* (New York, 1965).

Woods, G. F. "The Idea of the Transcendent," in A. R. Vidler, ed., *Soundings: Essays Concerning Christian Understanding* (Cambridge, 1963), pp. 43–65.

Wren, Christopher S. "An American Bishop's Search For A Space-Age God," *Look* (February, 1966).